DOUBLE PLAY

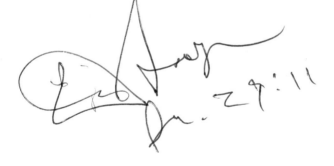

DAN HOOPER

DOUBLE PLAY
Copyright © 2007 by Dan Hooper

Unless otherwise noted, Scripture quotations are from the Holy Bible, New Living Translation. Copyright © 1996 by Tyndale House Publishers, Inc. Used by permission.

Scripture quotations marked KJV are from The Holy Bible, King James Version.

Scripture quotations marked NIV are from the Holy Bible, New International Version. Copyright © 1973, 1978, 1984, International Bible Society. Used by permission.

Scripture quotations marked NKJV are from the Holy Bible, New King James Version. Copyright © 1982 by Thomas Nelson, Inc., Nashville, TN. Used by permission.

Scripture quotations marked TLB are from The Living Bible. Copyright © 1971, Tyndale House Publishers, Inc. Used by permission.

All rights reserved. No part of this publication may be reproduced, stored in a retrieval system, or transmitted in any form by means electronic, mechanical, photocopying, recording or otherwise, except for the inclusion of brief quotations in a review, without prior permission in writing from the publisher.

ISBN: 0-9774223-4-8
978-0-9774223-4-0

Published by

LifeBridge
BOOKS
P.O. BOX 49428
CHARLOTTE, NC 28277

Printed in the United States of America.

Dedication

This book is solely dedicated to my best friend and life partner, Anna. After all these years together you are still the one I would rather be playing golf with, traveling with or just hanging out with than anyone else on the planet. I love doing life with you.

Contents

Chapter 1	The Road to Rediscovery	7
Chapter 2	Lighten Up!	17
Chapter 3	The Third Partner	33
Chapter 4	Men, Pay Attention!	51
Chapter 5	A Word to the Wives	63
Chapter 6	The Buffalo and the Butterfly	77
Chapter 7	How to Rekindle the Romance	91
Chapter 8	The Fidelity Factor	107
Chapter 9	Affair-Proof Your Marriage	123
Chapter 10	A Prosperous Partnership	145

Chapter One

The Road to Rediscovery

"I bet you were the class clown in high school," the gentleman commented, shaking my hand as he was leaving an early morning seminar for men. My topic that day was, "What Your Mother Couldn't Tell You That Your Daddy Didn't Know."

In my reply, I told him I considered the class clown in my school to be the guy who ran through the cafeteria during the lunch break wearing nothing but a football helmet and tennis shoes!

I quickly, added, "It wasn't me, but I was the one who talked 'that guy' into doing it."

Don't panic! My purpose and passion in writing this book is not to "talk you into something" you will later regret. Rather, there is a far more important issue at stake. I want to lead you into taking your marriage relationship to a level you may have never before dreamed possible. Today, I want to convince you that your family life can reach the top of the happiness scale. Regardless of your personal history or how you have seen other marriages flounder in the past, yours can be amazingly different.

Help is Ahead

I'm fully aware the majority of people don't pick up a book titled *Marriage & Relationships* until theirs is perhaps on shaky ground. So, it wouldn't surprise me if you are feeling a little more than discouraged over your marital situation at this moment. But real help is on the way. You can—and should—enjoy a relationship which is mutually satisfying in every area. One where joy and laughter are commonplace, and blessings and abundance take precedence over what may be lacking.

I'm talking of a marriage which is experiencing God's power, protection and provision—a daily union that continues to grow stronger, closer, safer and is filled with pleasure and delight.

The Takeoff!

Just like jet fuel and acceleration are essential elements for an airplane to operate, laughter and joy play major roles in any marriage getting off the ground—and they are vital for keeping it flying high!

One of the problems facing couples who have been around each other for an extended period of time is they tend to neglect their best assets—what made the relationship special in the first place. Later, I will be dealing with the importance of *happiness factors* in your life and marriage, and how to turn your union into a treasure you would never want to part with.

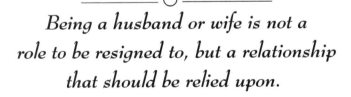

Being a husband or wife is not a role to be resigned to, but a relationship that should be relied upon.

Yet, the first thing you need to understand is that your Heavenly Father wants you to be happy. He deeply loves you and will never build a barrier between you and His blessings.

Does He Really Care?

After years of being a pastor, counselor and working with married couples of all ages, I have learned that many who are living out a bad existence together begin to think God must be punishing them. Somehow they conclude their relationship and happiness are not on His priority list. Such thinking couldn't be further from the truth.

It is our Heavenly Father who created the entire concept of marriage, sex and happiness in the first place!

---⊘---

The objective of marriage is not merely to <u>survive</u>, but to <u>thrive</u>; to become more effective and productive together than you could ever be or do separately.

God is not keeping anything of value or withholding what is profitable from your marriage, *"For the Lord God is our light and protector. He gives us grace and glory. No good thing will the Lord withhold from those who do what is right"* (Psalm 84:11).

Amazing Plans

Let me pose a few questions:

- Is having a happy, joyous relationship a *good thing?*
- Is owning a nice home a *good thing?*
- Is living in a marriage where you are not constantly arguing over money a *good thing?*
- Is being able to go on a vacation where you reconnect and build memories a *good thing?*

If you answered "yes" to the above, remember, God is not the one who is holding you back. His plans far exceed anything anyone could ever design for your life. He wants your love to grow and mature and for you to always cling to the belief your tomorrow will be more fulfilling as you live out His purpose.

Long ago, through the prophet Jeremiah, God declared, *"For I know the plans I have for you...plans to prosper you and not to harm you, plans to give you hope and a future"* (Jeremiah 29:11 NIV).

Broken Hearts

Out of the frustration of an unhappy marriage, don't ever say, "God must be mad at me!"

Let me stop you right there. No one has ever cared for you as much as your Heavenly Father. When you are hurting and your heart is broken, He certainly does not want you to remain in such a condition.

Like a glass container which is fractured or cracked, a broken heart will eventually spring a leak and leave room for the waters of discontent to creep in—such as low self-esteem, mistrust, skepticism, negativism and unforgiveness. These unhealthy emotions will invade your heart and cause your relationship unnecessary harm.

There's More!

Your married life doesn't have to be in a constant

state of turmoil, like those you see all around you, where just surviving seems to be the primary goal. You don't have to settle for second best. Your partnership can be revitalized with new energy, joy and objectives —where just getting through the day without another argument or trying to avoid spending too much time around your spouse, will be a thing of the past.

With the apostle Paul you can rejoice, *"Now glory be to God! By his mighty power at work within us, he is able to accomplish infinitely more than we would ever dare to ask or hope"* (Ephesians 3: 20).

A New Discovery

You are about to begin a new chapter in the life story of your relationship. No matter how hopeless you have felt or how far removed the reality of having a loving marriage has seemed, you can rediscover your first love—to desire more than anything else to be with the person you married and to have true love reciprocated.

Sadly, over the years I have talked with hundreds of couples who felt their marriage was over—where intimacy had come to a complete stop. Many had adulterous affairs, moved out and divided assets only to have a miracle of God reconnect their marriage. They became what they had never been before—best friends, mutually satisfying lovers and joy-filled people whose family and life flourished.

More than "Business Partners"

Yes, with the Lord's help you really can be blessed with both fun and favor in your marriage—one that is filled with laughter and prospering at the same time.

―――― ⊘ ――――
*You don't have to win at
work and lose at love.*

A union is so much more than being good business partners, paying the bills and running a taxi service for the kids.

You can experience both joy and abundance in every area of your marriage—a Double Play!

Jesus declares, *"The thief does not come except to steal, and to kill, and to destroy. I have come that they may have life, and that they may have it more abundantly"* (John 10:10 NKJV).

He Has the Answers

No one can force you to read on and apply these principles to your life:

- I can't talk your heart into *not* hurting.
- I can't convince your mind to forget painful words which have been shouted at you in the heat of an argument.
- I can't heal a wounded spirit or soothe your emotions into a state of calmness.

But I know the Person who can! I pray you will hear His voice as we continue this journey together.

Chapter Two

Lighten Up!

"Men are simple and women are complicated."

These are the opening words of my message to those attending our church one Sunday morning.

The statement was received with laughter and some friendly objection from those of the female gender in the auditorium. So I pushed forward, asking all the women to hold their purses high above their heads for a moment. They were more than happy to oblige and that's when I saw it—a purse the size of a backpack being held in the air by a woman on the second row whose name is Michele!

I asked, "Can I borrow your purse for a moment? I promise I won't look inside."

She readily handed it over and I held it up with one hand and announced to the people, "This is a woman and this (holding up my wallet in the other hand) is a man."

People enjoyed the visual illustration. One was a size which could probably hold everything a person would need for a two week vacation, while the man's wallet was just big enough to carry that day's allowance and a picture of his dog!

Decisions! Decisions!

I then placed the bag and the wallet side by side on the stage floor and continued the comparison. "A woman's entire life is more complex than a man's," I told the congregation. "For instance, when women were getting ready to come to church this morning they had a multitude of decisions to make. 'Should I wear a dress—or pants with a blouse? Perhaps jeans or dress slacks. Should I be casual or maybe a little dressier? Should I wear my hair up or down, straight or wavy? What kind of shoes will match? High heels, medium heels or flats—open toes or closed? What accessories should I add to this outfit?'"

The decisions go on and on—all this just to be able

to leave the house!

Men Have it Easy!

On the other hand, a man will pick up a shirt, look at it and if there is no sign of visible dirt he will then sniff it. If it does not smell funky, he will announce to his wife, "I've got myself an outfit."

It is just that easy with men because they are simple.

Most women have a tendency to over-analyze men. They are trying too hard to figure us out.

On with my observations! Young girls grow up playing house and communicating with each other —and for this reason are better at it than men. As a small boy growing up I never once heard one of my buddies say, "Let's go over to my house and braid hair and just talk."

If someone *had* said that to me, you can bet your week's salary I would have fled!

Towels and Pillows

I am not familiar with your linen closet, but in our house today we have an abundance of towels. We have towels which match other towels and those that match the walls. We have towels we use and those for display only—and a few strictly for visitors.

Now, if I were living by myself, I would only own two towels. One would be damp and the other would be dry. I would alternate them for six months. Then I would throw both of them out and buy myself two new towels!

Remember, as a man I am a simple soul. I have one head, one bed and one pillow. But on our bed we have eleven pillows! On my side I remove five of them every night and put five back every morning.

You may ask, "Why do you do that?"

There is only one reason; I am married to a woman!

"Oh, No!"

That Sunday morning, after sharing my thoughts, I held up the original large purse I had borrowed from

Michele. I asked her, "Is this your only purse?"

She smiled and answered, "Oh, no!"

I could not resist chiding her, "Of course not. Michele has *lots* of purses. Big purses, small purses, purses that match shoes and purses that match jewelry. Summer purses, spring purses, purses you carry over your shoulder and those you clutch with one hand."

Then, holding up my small wallet for all to see, I asked the question, "How many wallets does a man have?"

The entire congregation laughingly answered, "One!"

I finished by adding, "And a man will hang onto that one tattered wallet until a woman buys him a new one!"

Our Amusing Spouse

Well, it's easy to understand a woman, if you are a woman and it is easy to understand a man, if you are a man. The problems surface when we try to figure each other out. Yet, our differences can turn into a humorous adventure if we will all just relax and lighten up a little.

It's okay for us to not only appreciate the contrasts between men and woman but to also find them amusing, even comical, from time to time.

The last thing a woman ever wants to do is feminize her husband and her spouse certainly doesn't want his wife to act or think like a macho construction worker.

The Cement of Our Relationship

I married Anna, my high school sweetheart—a beautiful brown-eyed brunette from Fort Worth, Texas. We started out as acquaintances and soon became best friends.

She definitely has had her challenges over the years learning to understand this project-driven, people-person husband she married. And I certainly had to learn to appreciate this very peaceful and meticulous female in whose house I am privileged to live.

We both began a relationship with our Savior before

we met each other, and to this day our trust and faith in the Lord has only grown stronger. Without question it has been our deep love and commitment to God and His grace working in our lives—as individuals and a couple—that has brought our marriage and family through every challenge with great blessings and victory.

However, if you were to ask either of us, "What has been the one attribute the Lord has given you which has proven to be most effective in cementing your relationship together—both as friends and lovers?" the answer would unanimously be one word: "Laughter!"

We keep the "fun factor" alive and well.

A Healthy Distraction

Think back with me for a moment. What attracted you and your spouse in the beginning was not the hope of having someone to share driving the kids to soccer fields and gymnastics classes. Nor was the objective to add another income so you could pay the bills.

The most appealing factor at the start of your relationship was that the other person appeared fun to be around.

You were enamored with the fact he or she smiled and laughed—and could take your mind away from whatever troubles you may have been facing that week. In essence, the *attraction* was your ability to cause a *distraction* from your problems.

This same characteristic, if it hasn't been lost along the way, is the magnet which keeps drawing you closer through the years.

Delight in and celebrate this God-given ability to take your spouse away from stress, worry and the anxiety of living. Far away from the mundane routines of laundry, grocery shopping, yard work, cleaning, and raising the kids.

Don't get me wrong. I love doing yard work and helping Anna every way possibly I can, but I still desperately need a girlfriend and my wife needs a boyfriend to add an exciting alternative to everything predictable and expected.

What I Signed Up For

I pastor a wonderful group of people in Colorado, have a tremendous staff and an extremely busy personal schedule, but I still need my girlfriend!

My wife, Anna, is not only a grandmother of four, she is also a partner with me in overseeing the many ministry programs and staff of our church. Yet, she still needs her boyfriend! Being such a friend was the first job I signed up for, and it remains the most important one to this day.

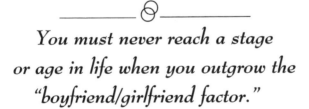

You must never reach a stage or age in life when you outgrow the "boyfriend/girlfriend factor."

If this is missing in a marriage you both will become vulnerable to a lifelong sadness and be robbed of the joy God desires.

The Best and Worst

Over the years I have had the privilege of conducting seminars, conferences and retreats for husbands and wives who wanted to improve their marriages. And in our church I address the issues of relationships and family life on a regular basis.

In counseling and dealing confidentially with private matters couples are facing, I've seen the absolute best and worst of partnerships.

Many of these marriages were on the brink of disaster, yet they rose from the dead, so to speak.

Conversely, I have witnessed many relationships where there was so much damage, rather than going through the painful process of repair, one or both of them would decide to simply give up.

The Missing Link

I look back at the wedding ceremonies I have performed for couples who were madly in love with each other—the ones who would stay on the phone for hours just to hear the other person breathe, without a thought in the world of wanting to end the call! The kind of young, ardent love and romance you see in classic movies.

I've watched them over the years as they have built careers, had children and raised a family. Yet, after gaining so much, there are those who suddenly feel something is missing—and they selfishly throw away what they have tried to establish together.

Without the fun and excitement of the young love you once knew in the early dating stage, what you have worked so hard for will disappear, leaving you empty and lonely.

I am convinced affairs are not the result of a husband or wife wanting to find another person they can have sex with as much as it is a craving for someone with whom they can share fun—and escape from the boredom at home.

How Men are "Wired"

In the past 30 years I have recommended many

books to men, women and couples. Most husbands do not enjoy reading as much as their wives—unless the material is of particular interest to them. So I keep that in mind when I promote a book, especially to a non-recreational reader.

I would like to suggest three titles which I believe can help you understand the heart and needs of your spouse.

First, every woman who genuinely wants to discover how God "wired" her husband, needs to read a book that was actually written by a man for men. It's *Wild at Heart*, by John Eldredge. On the back cover you'll read these words: "Every man was once a boy. And every little boy has dreams, big dreams: dreams of being the *hero*, of beating the bad guys, of doing daring feats and rescuing the damsel in distress. Every little girl has dreams, too: of being rescued by her prince and swept up into a great adventure, knowing that she is the *beauty*."

Once a guy starts reading this, I doubt he can put it down—and when a woman grasps its contents, she will begin to really understand the heart and inner desires of almost every male.

Our Basic Needs

Second, every couple should read together, *His Needs, Her Needs: Building An Affair Proof Marriage,* by Willard F. Harley, Jr.

Written in simple language, you will find the five basic needs of every woman and the five basic needs of every man. These are explained in a way where men can begin to fully grasp how important affection is to a woman and the cement of the relationship—how it symbolizes security, protection, comfort and approval, builds her self-worth and gives her confidence in every area.

I have given this book to almost every couple I have married or counseled in the last ten years. I highly recommend you only read two chapters together, then discuss the contents. Once you have a complete knowledge of these basic needs, you can move on to the next two chapters.

The Grass Isn't Greener

Third, every man and woman in a marriage where

one or both are unhappy, vulnerable and feeling like what they really want might be somewhere else, needs to read, *The Myth Of Greener Grass*, by J. Allen Petersen.

Moving on to another relationship, won't solve your problem. If you are struggling to find satisfaction in your present marriage, you won't find it in the next one either.

This insightful book will also help any couple who is recovering from an extra-marital affair, whether caused *by* you or *to* you.

Don't Miss the Joy

The common denominator running through all of these titles is the importance of not losing one of your greatest assets and attractions as a man or woman; what I call "the fun factor."

The practical help and advice I want to share in the

chapters which follow are designed to spark abundance and growth in your marriage, but if you miss the ingredient of joy in the relationship, your partnership is not complete.

Giddy love is not just for teenagers! Your husband needs a girlfriend. Your wife needs a boyfriend. Who do you want to fill that position?

Chapter Three

The Third Partner

During a period of over eight years in our ministry, Anna and I were totally involved in marriage counseling. In fact, there was hardly an evening when we were not working with couples from 17 to 70—and every age in between.

In the process, we established a "contract" between those we counseled and ourselves. We required both the husband and wife to come to the session having done their "homework"—based on the study of certain biblical principles. They were also expected to pray together every day concerning their circumstances.

More often than not, I would open the session by asking, "Did you do your homework this week?"

If the husband or wife responded, "No, we just didn't have time," I would say, "Well, we'll see you next week."

Or, I would ask, "Did the two of you pray together every night?"

Again, if the answer was, "No," I'd respond, "See you next week!"

In many cases, I found out my wife and I were committing more time to their relationship than they were.

For married couples who want to make their marriage work, it involves more than a few counseling sessions. It likely has taken years to unravel the relationship—and it's not going to be patched up by simply reading a book, attending a seminar or listening to the advice of someone else. It is only when you apply the information and make the decision to communicate with your spouse on critical matters that change is possible. Yes, homework is involved!

"I Feel Helpless"

In counseling troubled marriages, the sentiment I have heard most often is, "I feel powerless to change." Or, "I feel helpless—and I don't know what to do to make things different."

I wholeheartedly agree. I'm convinced you will not enjoy a mutually satisfying long-lasting union without Christ and His wonder-working power.

An Unlimited Resource

Besides our relationship with Christ, the most satisfying and "fun" experiences in life are those which occur between a husband and wife. Yet, with the potential of the union being a success, the risk of failure also looms high.

Let me call your attention to a verse of Scripture that gives you the promise of an unlimited resource in your relationship. *"I pray also that the eyes of your heart may be enlightened in order that you may know the hope to which he has called you, the riches of his glorious inheritance in the saints, and his incomparably great power for us who believe"* (Ephesians 1:18-19).

Who is this incredible power for? Every individual—including married couples.

Even more, *"That power is like the working of his mighty strength, which he exerted in Christ when he raised him from the dead and seated him at his right hand in the heavenly realms, far above all rule and authority, power and dominion, and every title that can be given, not only in the present age but also in the one to come"* (Ephesians 1:19-21 NIV).

This resurrection force is the same divine strength God makes available to every husband and wife.

Since this is true, outside of adultery or abuse, I don't believe there are any "impossible" cases where a spouse should throw up his or her hands and announce, "It's over!"

I also want to clarify that in this book I have no intention of placing a guilt trip on you concerning relationships of the past—including a previous marriage.

We can't change yesterday, only what is taking place right now.

No matter how disastrous you think your situation

is, God's life-changing power can radically transform your mate into the most loving, godly individual you could ever hope to be married to. And He can also change you!

She Called His Bluff!

Recently we dealt with a couple where the wife finally had enough and announced, "That's it! I am out of here!" She left the relationship.

We had tried to encourage and motivate him to attend church, but he always had an excuse for not being there. But when his wife walked out of the marriage, it shook him to his core. So much so, he was now standing on the church steps before the doors were even open. He couldn't get there fast enough. Why? Because she called his bluff and left!

Now, as a contrite soul, he would say, "If anybody can get our marriage back together, Christ can."

We watched as he said all the right things and made all the correct moves. In my observation, if I told him to do a back-flip in the middle of the aisle, he would do it—anything to reconcile with his estranged wife.

After hours and months of counseling she finally admitted, "I think I see a ray of hope. He seems willing to go to church and make some changes. There is more of a sensitivity and compassion."

So she reunited with him and together they attended church for a few weeks—then he slowly reverted back to his old habits. We didn't see him in the services.

Sadly, the second time she left it was for keeps!

I can't begin to tell you how many times I have seen this scenario repeated.

How Can We Know?

I am convinced it takes three to make a marriage successful: the husband, the wife and God.

You can have all the instruction in the world, however, if you leave the Lord out of the intimate equation of marriage, you're not going to make it.

How can God help? He can give you the power to fathom the differences between you and your mate. The word "fathom" means to understand the *depth* of something.

I hear people say:

- "Well, I just don't understand him."
- "I can't figure her out!"
- "Why does he act like this?"

It's natural to come to these conclusions. This is why the apostle Paul told the believers at Corinth, *"No one can really know what anyone else is thinking or what he is really like, except that person himself"* (I Corinthians 2:11 TLB).

In fact, what we do know about God Himself are the things He reveals to us (v.12).

Here's the bottom line. The only way the husband can possibly understand the wife's differences is for her to tell him what they are—and vice versa. The husband must explain his needs in a way she can fully comprehend.

What About Our Differences?

Before marriage, we are so blinded by love and emotion the only thing we notice about our future spouse is our *similarities.*

This was certainly true of Anna and me. I was convinced we liked the same kind of movies and music, and enjoyed the same type of food. If was only after we were married I learned she really didn't like fish!

Yes, love really is blind!

If I asked you to name two major opposites between you and your mate, what would they be? Would they involve personality traits? Separate interests?

God certainly must have a sense of humor the way He brings some couples together:

- One may be an early bird—the other a night owl.
- One may be cautious—the other takes risks.
- One may love to talk—the other more quiet or reserved.
- One may love to spend money—the other is a tightwad!

- One may love to cuddle—the other is less tactile or physical.
- Regarding sex, one may be a microwave oven—the other a slow cooker!
- One may always be on time—the other "flexible."

These contrasts don't mean one is always right and the other wrong. No, we are just different.

Here is what God's Word says concerning the matter: *"... husbands must give honor to your wives. Treat your wife with understanding as you live together. She may be weaker than you are, but she is your equal partner in God's gift of new life. Treat her as you should so your prayers will not be hindered"* (1 Peter 3:7).

And this is written to both the husband and wife, *"Finally, all of you should be of one mind. Sympathize with each other. Love each other as brothers and sisters. Be tenderhearted, and keep a humble attitude"* (v.8).

The Wisdom Factor

The bridge between our uniqueness can be crossed only through wisdom and understanding. As King Solomon wrote long ago, *"By wisdom a house is built, and through understanding it is established"* (Proverbs 24:3 NIV).

You may say, "I've tried, but I must not have what it takes."

Don't give up! The answer is much closer than you realize.

James tells us, *"If any of you lacks wisdom, let him ask of God, who gives to all liberally and without reproach, and it will be given to him"* (James 1:5 NKJV).

The only way you can gain wisdom for *anything* you must deal with is to ask the Almighty. However, you have been given the ability to obtain understanding and knowledge on your own—through diligent study.

As I recently told a gentleman who was searching for answers, "You ask God for everything else; yet, when was the last time you prayed for wisdom?"

Your Source of Power

Through the years I have come to learn that the closer I am to the Lord, the closer I am to my wife. To put it another way, there is no way on earth I can be a jerk to Anna and be in tune with God! And I can't be consistent in my prayer life and be inconsiderate of her.

This brings me to this important principle:

> God can give us the power to
> fulfill our mates's needs.

Remember, it was the Creator who designed marriage, sex and families.

Scripture declares, *"The husband should fulfill his marital duty to his wife, and likewise the wife to her husband. The wife's body does not belong to her alone but also to her husband. In the same way, the husband's body does not belong to him alone but also to his wife"* (1 Corinthians 7:3-4 NIV).

It is both the husband's and wife's responsibility to meet their mates needs.

Many women want their husband to fulfill their emotional and physical requirements, yet expect him to instinctively know what they are, without having to tell him—expecting him to figure it out.

As a result men and women are struggling in the dark, trying to meet the desires of their spouse based on their own personal needs. However, that's not the way it works.

Tell Her! Tell Him!

As a newly married husband, I didn't have a clue! My dad and I had no father-son talk and I went into the relationship thinking, "Whatever makes me emotionally, mentally and physically happy, I will just do the same things for Anna."

Boy, did I miss the mark!

The only way we can know how to meet what our spouse requires is to ask.

Ladies, be open, honest and tell him what you desire! Sir, she won't know your needs if you fail to communicate.

The Kiss!

I smiled when I heard about a husband and wife who were in marriage counseling with a secular psychologist. The wife was upset and sat there with her arms folded.

The counselor was frustrated, but continued to reach out to her.

This went on for at least an hour and a half. Then the weary psychologist walked over to the woman and planted a big kiss on her cheek. He took her by the hands, looked her in the eyes and tenderly asked, "How are you hurting?"

She immediately began to cry and started talking —melting like a marshmallow.

A few minutes later, the marriage counselor looked over at the husband and said, "I'm telling you, that kiss represents what your wife needs every single day of her life."

The surprised husband replied, "I can have her down here on Tuesdays and Thursdays!"

Whose Interests?

Meeting your mate's needs is a skill which must be learned—it doesn't happen automatically.

I'm convinced at least eighty percent of marital issues would be erased if we would "live out" this verse: *"Let each of you look out not only for his own interests, but also for the interests of others"* (Philippians 2:4 NKJV).

"His Good Purpose"

The number one problem I encounter in marriage relationships is that of selfishness.

I hear husbands and wives indignantly exclaim, "I've got to do what's best for me."

The man of the house is somehow convinced, "If I'm okay and my career is doing well then the relationship will be great"—while their mate is lonely and emotionally falling apart.

Here is what is taking place. The husband goes to work and does his best to provide. But in a "needs-meeting" relationship, there is no energy left to sustain the marriage. Yet, he continues to think, "I work and bring home a paycheck so she can buy what she needs. I do this to show how much I love her."

Both husbands and wives need to understand that God will give you whatever is required to make your marriage one of love and fulfillment—including the ability, energy and time to meet the needs of your spouse.

The Bible tells us, *"...for it is God who works in you to will and to act according to his good purpose"* (Philippians 2:13 NIV). Your Heavenly Father will not ask you or your spouse to do anything He does not empower you to do.

This is why it is impossible to consistently meet your mate's needs through your own efforts. You're going to grow weary in the process. It can only be accomplished through God's unlimited power.

Your Options

Here are two laws of reality you'd better come face to face with:

1. You married an imperfect person.
2. You're not so hot yourself!

In the course of your marriage, you and your spouse are going to make mistakes which will upset the other person. And when this happens you have one of two options: (1) you can take that mistake and rub it in, or (2) you can rub it out!

Wipe the Slate Clean

This brings me to a divine truth:

God can give you the power to forgive your mate's mistakes.

What does Scripture tell us? *"Get rid of all*

bitterness, rage, anger, harsh words, and slander, as well as all types of evil behavior. Instead, be kind to each other, tenderhearted, forgiving one another, just as God through Christ has forgiven you" (Ephesians 4:31-32).

Don't grow resentful and stubbornly hold on to past hurts and rejections. *"Make allowance for each others faults, and forgive anyone who offends you. Remember, the Lord forgave you, so you must forgive others"* (Colossians 3:13).

If your marriage is going to thrive and be successful, wipe the slate clean and start over by making God your Third Partner.

Chapter Four

Men, Pay Attention!

As a kid, one of my favorite television shows was called *Lost in Space*. It revolved around a family known as the Robinsons—Professor John, his wife Maureen and their three children, Judy, Penny and Will.

They were the world's first space family, sent to colonize a distant planet. I can still remember the "pet" they had in this desolate land; it was a robot!

Whenever the robot saw something that didn't make sense to him, he would start waving his arms and shout, "Danger! Alien Approaching!"

Today, when it comes to understanding women, men often view the subject the same way: "Danger! Alien Approaching!" These are creatures they just can't quite figure out.

Sigmund Freud, widely known as the "father of psychoanalysis," once observed, "The great question that has never been answered, and which I have not yet been able to answer, despite my thirty years of research into the feminine soul, is 'What does a woman want?'"

While females are complex creations, the Bible says God made both man and woman in His image.

The Almighty formed each gender differently, yet He does not expect us to relate to each other like some mindless robot from outer space.

Instead, He desires for us to understand and meet the needs of our spouses.

Her Five Great Needs

One of the most significant gifts we can give women —whether it be our moms, our mates or our daughters—is a deeper understanding of them.

Let me share five specific requirements of the

woman you married:

1. Your Wife Needs Verbal Communication

At times, trying to exchange thoughts and ideas with your wife is similar to dealing with cell phone service in the mountains—it's full of static and the message doesn't always come through loud and clear.

Let's face facts: women are far better communicators than men. It's probably because they have more practice. After all, studies have shown the average woman speaks 12,000 more words each day than the average man. So, when the weary husband arrives home from work and only has 100 words left in his verbal tank, his wife may have several thousand!

Men, we have much to learn from our wives on this topic.

There are times I will come home in the evening and Anna will be anxious to discuss an issue with me. For example, it may concern a particular person she thinks would be excellent for a special ministry in the church. Instead of listening or exchanging ideas, I will quickly interrupt and ask her, "Why don't you call and find out if they're ready to help?"

You see, most men think logically and want to get right to the point: "Bring me a problem and I'll solve it." Women, however, would rather talk it out.

The "Feeling" Level

I have to constantly remind myself that communicating with a woman is not about reaching a particular goal, fixing what's broken or coming to a solution. The objective is the communication itself.

She is not looking for my advice, rather a person who will explore the subject. It is not my mouth she needs, but my shoulder! To her, verbal expression is a goal in itself.

Women want us to communicate with them on a "feeling" level. Not for us to hurriedly say, "Honey, try this," rather to express, "Here's what my heart tells me concerning the matter."

Take 20!

Men, let me suggest this homework assignment.

Starting tonight, after you get the kids to bed, turn off the television and just talk to your wife for the next 20 minutes.

She may do 80 percent of the talking, but that's okay. Tune in and listen. You may think 20 minutes is a long time, but she probably doesn't consider it long enough!

Don't try to "fix" her or change her thinking on whatever subject you are discussing. Just look her in the eyes and concentrate on what she is saying.

If you want to have health and progress in your marriage—or in any other area of your life—learn what it means to have meaningful communications. Scripture tells us, *"An unreliable messenger stumbles into trouble, but a reliable messenger brings healing"* (Proverbs 13:17).

2. YOUR WIFE NEEDS EMOTIONAL SUPPORT

From time to time men tell me, "Pastor, you're trying to get me in tune with my emotions, share things with my wife and make me a 'soft' type of a person."

That is exactly right!

A husband once exclaimed, "But I grew up in a non-expressive home and never saw a man really expose his feelings or emotions. And since I was raised this way, it's just how I am."

Well, get over it!

Women believe emotional support is the cement which holds the relationship together. As a result, they need for a man to be able to "talk out" how he feels, not just what he knows. King Solomon said, *"...share your love only with your wife"* (Proverbs 5:15).

The majority of men have been trained to be overcomers, conquerors, achievers and providers—not to be conversationalists. But remember, the Bible counsels husbands to *"...love your wives and never treat them harshly"* (Colossians 3:19).

Watch Your Words

Guys have a hard time relating to this, because

when we are socializing with other men we say whatever we think. On the golf course, after a lousy shot, I've heard one buddy tell another, "Hey, if you can't hit the ball any better than that, maybe you ought to move up to the women's tees!"

A man will chide his friend, "You need to start doing some exercises, your stomach is almost as big as a beach ball."

Now if a woman were to be that blunt to another woman, the friendship would probably come to a screeching halt!

Not so with men. They can cut each other to shreds one minute and be slapping backs the next!

This is why the Bible tells you not to use harsh words with your wife. They don't recover from hurts as quickly as you—and desperately need your emotional support.

A Three-Pointer?

I grew up playing basketball, and when we were first married I thought there were certain things I could do that would be like a three-point shot. For example, I believed if I took Anna out to an expensive restaurant or bought her a beautiful piece of jewelry—swoosh!

Three points! Or, a luxury vacation at an exotic destination. Another three on the scoreboard!

In my mind, I was convinced that if I was falling behind in demonstrating my love and attention, I could make up for it in a hurry by making a big splash.

However, with women, this is not their rationale. To them, everything is one point—regardless of whether it is a special holiday or a simple Hallmark card. What she loves is not merely the extravagant surprises we arrange to make up for our stupid errors, rather those little acts we demonstrate on a regular basis.

3. Your Wife Needs to be Nurtured

Men, don't leave your leadership and creativity at the workplace, then come home and put yourself in neutral. Be involved with your family and constantly nurture your wife.

This is vital, because, *"...a man who loves his wife actually shows love for himself"* (Ephesians 5:28)—and as a result you both develop and flourish.

―――――― ⌬ ――――――

Never forget, the woman you married was God's daughter before she became your wife.

By taking her as your partner you have also accepted the responsibility for her continual care. This is why you are to nurture and sustain her all the days of your life.

4. YOUR WIFE NEEDS A MAN WITH PURPOSE

Women want to be hooked up with a man whose life transcends the temporal—who has a greater calling than just mending fences, pulling weeds and watching the New York Yankees or Dallas Cowboys on television on weekends.

Your wife desires a man who knows Christ and whose life is driven with a divine purpose to make a difference in the lives of others. As a pastor, I know how proud a woman is of her spouse when he is involved in ushering, teaching a class, or any other ministry of the church.

God tells us, *"I have appointed you for the very purpose of displaying my power in you"* (Romans 9:17).

There are occasions when you need to be strong, and other times where softness is required. Ask the Lord to give you the wisdom to discern the difference.

Through the years of our marriage, there have been days when Anna needed me to be tender-hearted, and other times tough as nails! For example, when our children were small, she delighted in seeing me lovingly care for them when I came home from the office. On some days, if they were behaving badly, and she had been struggling with them, she expected me to step in and become the disciplinarian.

5. Your Wife Needs Security

You don't have to be wealthy to provide financial stability in your home. A wife is looking for a husband who is committed to his work and willing to build a strong economic base for the family.

Scripture declares, *"...those who won't care for...those in their own household, have denied the true faith. Such people are worse than unbelievers"* (1 Timothy 5:8).

Men, God has placed the responsibility of being a bread-winner on us. If your wife works, she is to be commended for what she does. But the crux of the matter remains, the Lord is looking to you to take care of the financial provision of the family. This means you may have to take on extra work to meet the budget.

The ball is in your court. Regardless of the sacrifice, continue to declare, *"I can do all things through Christ who strengthens me"* (Philippians 4:13 NKJV).

When you partner with God financially, you will meet the economic needs of your spouse as well.

What's Your Score?

Let me give you a quick test. We have discussed five "needs" you are to provide for your wife, but I have not presented them in order of priority.

Before reading any further, I want you to look at these again and rank them from the most important on down. What's on your priority list?

According to studies, the five basic needs in a woman's life are—from highest to lowest:

1. Emotional support.
2. Verbal communication.
3. Financial security.
4. A nurturing husband.
5. A man with an ultimate purpose.

One more question. If your wife were to grade you on each of these qualities, where would you stand? Which category would be excellent? Satisfactory? Needs improvement?

Don't gloss over your deficiencies. Ask God to help you make the necessary changes today.

Chapter Five

A Word to the Wives

I once heard an amusing story about a man and woman who grew tired of living with all the congestion, smog and traffic prevalent in the city and decided to move out west and buy a cattle ranch.

One of the first decisions this city slicker and his family had to make was what they were going to call their new ranch. The husband recalled "I wanted to name it 'The Flying W,' but my wife wanted 'The Suzy Q.'" And he added, "One of my sons liked 'Bar J' and my other son suggested we should name the ranch, 'Lazy Y.'"

A visitor to the property who was listening to the story, looked around and didn't see any livestock. "What happened to your cattle?" he asked.

The owner exclaimed, "Oh, unfortunately, none of them survived the branding!"

Like this family, some people can't agree on anything.

What Makes Him Tick?

In a successful marriage, different viewpoints must be reconciled—at the same time realizing and respecting the unique individuals we truly are.

We have discussed several differences between male and female, but nowhere is it more pronounced than in a biological matter called testosterone, the principle male sex hormone which runs through a man's body.

Women have this hormone too, but in much smaller doses. On average, a male produces approximately twenty to thirty times as much testosterone as does a female. Since this is a medical fact, a wife needs to know how high, medium or low testosterone levels will affect her husband.

I mention this to illustrate the wide disparity between the physical and emotional needs of husbands and wives—and how each must understand what makes the other tick.

Let me share four basic needs of your husband, which only you can supply:

1. YOUR HUSBAND NEEDS A WELL-MANAGED HOME

One of the primary requirements of a man is to live in a house which is a refuge, not a place of disorder and chaos.

The Bible tells us it is the woman's responsibility to be the manager of the home: *"She carefully watches everything in her household and suffers nothing from laziness"* Proverbs 31:27).

We are also instructed, *"...older women must train the younger women to love their husbands and their children, to live wisely and be pure, to work in their homes"* (Titus 2:4-5).

This daily assignment must be approached as a joy rather than a drudgery or duty. As Solomon wrote, *"Better a dry crust eaten in peace than a house filled with feasting—and conflict"* (Proverbs 17:1).

The wife's management of the household is no different than that of the executive who is responsible for operating a business or corporation.

Instead of personally doing all the work to sustain a smooth-sailing ship, she delegates and assigns the tasks to each member of the family.

Then, on a regular basis, there is an accountability session to make sure Robert, Mary, Bobby and Janie have all accomplished their designated assignments.

In this arrangement, the man is not superior to the woman, nor the wife lording it over her husband. Even though the husband is ordered in Scripture as the ultimate decision maker, we are all on a level playing field when it relates to our responsibilities.

More than a Maid!

Please understand, the woman's role as manager doesn't equate to "maid."

Regardless of who is in charge of a particular portfolio, there needs to be constant consultation. For example, if the husband manages the finances, he should never make a major expenditure without first discussing it with his spouse.

Marriage is a partnership.

Since I am an inveterate people person, if I were managing our home, we'd probably have a party every night! I would tell my friends, "The barbecue is on. Bring your golf clubs and we'll chip a few balls in the backyard."

However, since Anna and I are a team, we balance each other out. It's her capable management that brings order and stability to our household.

2. Your Husband Needs to be Affirmed

The male species is actually far weaker than you think, and we crave your compliments and applause.

―――――― ⊗ ――――――
The reason we are the king of our castle is because you are the crown.

It's just the way God planned it to be: *"A worthy wife is a crown for her husband"* (Proverbs 12:4).

The fact she is by your side allows you to walk upright, with confidence—like royalty.

The husband who has an affirming wife will undertake projects in the workplace with assurance and belief because there is a woman at home who is encouraging. She is his cheerleader, saying, "I know you face some challenges, but you have the skills to work it out." Or, she may tell him, "Honey, I've never known you to quit on anything in your whole life."

With such positive support, a man feels he can conquer the world—and he can!

The opposite is also true. The Bible says, *"...a shameful wife saps his strength"* (Proverbs 12:4).

It's not surprising that a person who is continually berated at home starts doubting and telling himself, "I can't do this. I'll never get a better job. I am in debt and there's no hope in sight."

Three Principles

Wives, let me suggest you apply these three

suggestions in confirming and encouraging your husband:

One: The 48-Hour Principle

This means you don't allow a 48-hour period to pass by without complimenting your husband on a character trait—whether it is his humor, his leadership ability, his sensitivity, his smile, or whatever.

He doesn't necessarily have to be a Herculean champion in any of these areas, yet the very fact you are boosting his ego will cause him to make these virtues rise to the surface.

Two: The Audience Principle

When men perform in front of other people, suddenly they do everything at a higher level, even if it is an audience of one applauding, "That was good!"

Perhaps the most important group a man will ever stand before is his own children. This is why it's important for a wife to validate her husband in front of the family.

I can still remember the time I heard from my kids, "Mom thinks you're great, and so do we!"

Wow, I was walking on air!

Three: The "Special Gift" Principle

When Anna goes shopping in a city like Denver or Dallas, she may buy something for herself or an item for the house, but she never forgets me. I can't begin to count the times she has given me something she has personally picked out.

By presenting me with what is "special," it confirms the fact I am foremost in her thoughts.

3. YOUR HUSBAND NEEDS RECREATIONAL COMPANIONSHIP

Men desire a spouse who is playful and entertaining. I am convinced the majority of adulterous affairs do not begin because of sex—rather there is a craving for a person they can have fun with.

Has your relationship grown too serious, even boring? We are not created to just merely exist or tolerate life, but rather to relish every minute—to *"live happily"* with our spouse (Ecclesiastes 9:9).

It's been said, "The couple who prays together, stays together." Let me also suggest, "The couple who <u>plays</u> together stays together."

J. B. Phillips translates Colossians 3:18. *"Wives, adapt yourself to your husbands..."* There may be certain recreational activities he enjoys that perhaps you don't. Why not surprise him by exerting the effort and taking up the sport or learning more about his hobby.

Time to "Re-create"

Each of us have three "tanks" in life: spiritual, emotional and physical, and when they are depleted it leaves us running on empty.

To replenish any spiritual loss, we attend church, listen to worship music on a CD, or read the Bible while sipping a cup of coffee.

When you're exhausted physically, you take a nap until your energy is renewed.

But what is the plan of attack when the pain and discouragement of life drains your emotional batteries? This is when you need to re-create—or involve yourself in *recreation.*

Remember, your husband is just an overgrown boy, and he needs a toy to play with! Find an activity the two of you can enjoy together.

I remember the time Anna thought golfing was a rather stupid sport. Then one day she decided to join me by driving the cart while I chased the little white ball from the rough to the green.

It wasn't long, however, before she tried out my putter and finally got hooked on the sport. Today, it's one of our favorite activities together—she's now a golf fanatic!

One woman complained to me, "The way my husband loves hunting and fishing, I think he would like me better if I had antlers and fins!"

I advised her, "You need to seriously think about throwing a line in the water, too."

4. Your Husband Needs Sexual Fulfillment

At the marriage altar, the man who slipped the ring on your finger was publicly confirming, "For the rest of my life, I am only going to focus my attention, make love to and have my satisfaction from one body—yours!"

Let me pose this question: Other than you, what else will your husband spend the rest of his life with?

- Will he own just one car for the remainder of his days?
- Will he only purchase one suit for life?
- Will he have just one project to work on?
- Will he use the same tools or computer forever?

Only the woman he marries—and her body—is for keeps! This is how God intended it to be.

Not only does your husband have a responsibility in this area, so do you! Even more, why not learn to be an expert?

An Incredible Gift

Over the years I've counseled couples where the spouse confided, "Sex may be an important need to a man, but he married me and I'm going to change him!"

She somehow had come to the mistaken conclusion lovemaking was primarily to make the man happy.

Wrong! Sex is an incredible gift designed by God to be mutually satisfying.

I still remember a seminar Anna and I attended many years ago conducted by Dr. Ed Wheat, a medical doctor and author of *Intended for Pleasure*.

The man was in his 70s, and so was his wife, who was part of the session. At one point, she announced, "I want all you women to follow me." Several hundred wives walked to an adjoining auditorium.

On the way home, bursting with curiosity, I couldn't wait to ask Anna, "What did she tell you?"

Here was her message in a nutshell. "Women, make love to your husband whether you are in the mood or not—for two reasons. Number one, because it will help him be less grouchy. Number two, besides, it doesn't take that much time anyway!"

I had to really think about that!

One more Exam

At the end of the last chapter I asked the husbands to rank the needs of a wife from highest to lowest. Now it's time for wives to do the same with the four areas we've discussed.

What is your priority ranking?

According to most research, here is the correct order:

1. Sexual fulfillment.
2. Recreational companionship.
3. A managed household.
5. An affirming spouse.

What score do you give yourself in each of these areas? Perhaps it's time for some improvement!

Chapter Six

The Buffalo and the Butterfly

Have you ever seen a romantic animal? And I am not referring to George Clooney or Richard Gere!

In truth, all animals and insects have a romantic streak. How else can we account for the fact there are over one million species still multiplying today?

When you study their habits, some are strikingly similar to marriages. Let me give you a few examples.

She's a Widow!

The infamous black widow spider is approximately four times the size of her male counterpart. She is shiny and black, while he is much lighter in color.

She is virtually blind, yet knows every tiny detail of her silk web. So, when the male comes calling, he enters very gingerly—carefully stroking his hind legs on the web as if they were guitar strings. Then, after gently approaching, he finally ensnares her with his legs and a struggle ensues as they mate.

The now exhausted male attempts to leave, but stumbles and falls into the sticky web.

Immediately, the black widow's hunting instincts are triggered and she pounces on him. As reported by those who study spiders—she often kills and devours her mate!

I guess that's what makes her a widow!

Don't tell me your secrets, but you've probably encountered women whom you think have similar character traits!

Driven Away!

In the world of animals and insects, the spider isn't the only case where the husband is the weaker sex. For example, female elephants will hunt together, keeping the males at bay —except for a short mating season.

If a baby elephant is born and happens to be a male, he will remain with the females until he is a teenager, then is driven away to run with the other men.

The males may try to intermingle with the females, but are constantly rebuffed unless *she* accepts his advances and gets pregnant. Then he is sent off once more.

In far too many marriages today, the wife reigns over her husband through the force of her personality. As a result, there is constant confusion in the partnership.

The Dominating Male

In case you think it is all one-sided in the animal kingdom, let's look at a reverse situation. In southern Africa and parts of Asia there is an exotic bird known as the Pied Hornbill—whose bill resembles a cow's horn (but without the twist).

After mating with the female, he will fly above her, driving her into a cavity he has constructed from mud, droppings and fruit pulp. Once she enters this special little "apartment," he literally closes the hole and she can't leave until her eggs are hatched.

There is one small opening, just large enough for him to transfer food to the mother and the chicks.

Sadly, there are husbands who treat their wives in a similar manner—dominating and choking off her individuality, talents and gifts. With a powerful presence, and sometimes brute force, he squelches his spouse and makes all the decisions, letting her know, "I'm in charge around here!"

As one woman told me, "My husband is willing to have a 50-50 relationship—just as long as his half is the biggest!"

What a Snake!

If you want to find the original "love 'em and leave 'em" species, take a look at the rattlesnake.

The male rattler courts the serpent of his dreams by standing tall on his tail, swaying back and forth like an exotic dancer. The female responds by doing the same.

Yet, after they mate, the male leaves, never to

return again. Even after the baby rattlesnake is born, the offspring never sees its father.

This example in nature resembles those in the human realm who marry strictly for physical gratification. Then they go their separate ways with little or no care or communication.

In some cases, children are raised by nannies, sent to boarding schools and summer camps—never truly relating as a family.

Thankfully, this is not the pattern in *all* creatures of the animal kingdom. For example, the wolf and the penguin choose partners for life and are forever loyal to their mates and offspring.

The Power of Love

Our models for marriage, however, are not to be based on animal magnetism, but on the love which God demonstrated by sending His Son to earth. The most powerful words in human history are these: *"For God so loved the world, that he gave his only begotten Son, that whosoever believeth in him should not perish, but have everlasting life"* (John 3:16).

*Love is an action verb. If you give
love, you expect it to be reciprocated.*

Pay close attention to how the apostle Paul describes this special gift from above. *"Love is patient and kind. Love is not jealous or boastful or proud or rude. It does not demand its own way. It is not irritable, and it keeps no record of being wronged. It does not rejoice about injustice but rejoices whenever the truth wins out. Love never gives up, never loses faith, is always hopeful, and endures through every circumstance"* (1 Corinthians 13:4-7).

The Underlying Issue

I've counseled those who say, "Pastor I have an anger management problem." Or, "I'm always losing my temper."

This is not an anger issue, it's a love problem. Rudeness and affection are incompatible—and the person who is truly in love will tame his temper and hold his tongue.

Knowing these are driving principles:

- How can a man treat his neighbor better than he does his wife?
- How can he show more sensitivity and concern for his secretary at the office than to the woman he made a vow to love for better or for worse?
- How can he demonstrate more consideration and kindness to a pet or a stranger than his own children?

Of all the marvelous gifts our Heavenly Father has given us, none has a higher value. This is why we must give it first place in our marriage. As Paul states, *"Three things will last forever—faith, hope, and love—and the greatest of these is love"* (v.13).

Are You Vulnerable?

Men, learn to be transparent and honest with your wife. Instead of being the strong, silent type—like

Clint Eastwood—open up a little!

In the home, the woman gives both physically and emotionally, and she deserves for you to respond in the same manner.

This means you must allow her to see beneath the macho persona you may try to project. Become vulnerable.

If you have ever been wounded in a relationship, exposing your innermost feelings can be difficult, yet love which flows from the heart and is personally expressed, is what your wife deserves and expects.

Develop Your Skills

I've met men who fail to take advantage of Valentine's Day, neglecting to send their wife cards or flowers. This is an annual opportunity you should never miss!

Your wife will cherish a simple handwritten note which reads, "Honey, I really love you."

Avoid being like the man I heard about who complained, "I don't know what I'm going to get my wife for Christmas. She hasn't even used the floor sander I bought her last year!"

Many outdoor types have studied scores of books to develop their skills as a hunter, yet they've never read one manual on improving their techniques as a husband.

Just because you have obtained a hunting license doesn't mean you are the world's expert on hunting.

The same is true after the wedding. The fact you were issued a marriage license is no proof you instantly become an authority on being a husband. You need to study the art of maintaining romance in your partnership.

The "Love Quotient"

In one counseling session, in front of her husband,

a rather distraught wife told me, "In the last four years, my husband has never touched me once, other than for wanting sex."

I thought she was exaggerating. So I gave him a chance to respond, asking, "Surely you have held her hand or put your arm around her shoulder."

Looking down at the floor, he said, "I was raised in a family that didn't show affection, and I guess it's my nature, too." He added, "I never saw my mom and dad kiss each other—and not once did my father hug or tell me he loved me, or how proud he was of my accomplishments."

The wife, however, had been raised in a family which was just the opposite. They were demonstrative huggers, encouragers, and "lovers."

Thankfully, after these two shared their feelings there was a marked improvement their LQ—the "Love Quotient" of their relationship

If you are not the affectionate type—whether husband or wife—you had better learn to change. There is no option in this area.

Ask yourself, "Where do I rank on the affection scale?"

Pieces of the Puzzle

One fact I have learned after performing hundreds of marriage ceremonies and even more counseling sessions is that most couples think their problems are unique. Not so. Your conflicts are no different than those taking place in other homes.

Although I am a firm believer in godly counsel, the vast majority of couples could save themselves hours of grief if they would make a commitment to calmly and prayerfully communicate their needs to one another.

Tone down the temper. Stop and listen to what your spouse is saying. Then resolve to work on one issue at a time until the pieces of the puzzle fall back into place.

Sensitive or Tough?

Men, your wife resembles a butterfly.

Women, your husband is much like a buffalo.

Butterflies are beautiful creatures, but at the slightest provocation, they can be frightened and fly away. They are attracted to colorful flowers and are conscious of the "little things" in life, yet they are difficult to catch.

However, if you took a small pebble and placed it on the wing of a delicate butterfly, it wouldn't be able to lift off the ground—and in a panic may even lose its life

What a difference compared to the mighty buffalo. Even if he were facing a 30 or 40-mile-an-hour wind, he would hardly notice.

As for flowers, he'd probably stomp on them rather than eat them. And if a pebble were placed on his back, he wouldn't even know it was there.

Butterflies are sensitive while buffalos are tough. Yet, in comparing these creatures to a marriage, the analogy breaks down. Why? Because in the world of nature, the buffalo can never relate to the butterfly, or vice versa.

In a God-blessed marriage, however, that tough man (the buffalo) can begin to develop affection, sensitivity and kindness. He can learn to understand and appreciate the delicacies of his wife (the butterfly). In turn, she can begin to prize the inner drives and masculinity of her husband. As a result there can be a fulfilling relationship.

"What Would You Do?"

I remember meeting with a couple where the wife was trying her best to heal the rift, but her husband acted totally disinterested. In most cases, this is the the way the encounters usually begin—it's primarily the wife who does the initiating.

When I was finally able to gain his attention, I asked, "What if a van pulled up in your driveway and two thugs jumped out, grabbed your wife and kids, forced them into their vehicle and were about to drive off. What would you do?"

Thinking for a moment, the man replied, "It couldn't happen?"

"Why, I asked.

"Because, I'd tackle those guys before they ever had a chance. And if they did get them in the van, I would smash the windshield to keep them from escaping. I'd do whatever it takes."

"Sir," I told him, "if you don't deal with the issues we are talking about, the end result will be the same. Your wife and children will be gone. Is that what you want?"

He began to cry—and it was the start of a miraculous healing in their marriage and home.

As God's creatures, we need to suppress our self-centered desires and demonstrate His marvelous love.

Chapter Seven

How to Rekindle the Romance

A letter was written to the popular newspaper columnist, "Dear Abby," which stated the following: "Do all marriages go stale after 25 years? Ours has. My husband and I don't seem to have much to converse about any more? We used to talk about our kids, but now they're grown and gone. I have no major complaints concerning my husband, but the flame of excitement is gone. We watch a lot of television, read quite a bit and have friends drop by. But after they have left and we are alone, things are pretty dull. We even sleep in separate bedrooms now. Is there some way to recapture the old magic?"

The letter was signed, "The Song Has Ended."

How sad, yet she was expressing the heartache of

millions of wives.

In a survey of couples who had been married more than twenty years, the number one response was, "We don't seem to love each other the way we used to?"

Going Through the Motions?

What do you do when your marriage has lost its pazzaz? What happens when the relationship has fizzled and there's no more sparkle?

You may find it surprising, but Jesus gives us the answers to these questions.

As part of John's revelation, Christ detailed specific instructions to His bride—the church. As husbands and wives we need to follow His divine counsel.

Jesus asked John to give this message to the believers at Ephesus, *"I know all the things you do. I have seen your hard work and your patient endurance...But I have this complaint against you. You don't love me or each other as you did at first! Look how far you have fallen! Turn back to me and do the works you did at first"* (Revelation 2:2,4-5).

Christ was telling the believers, "You're going

through the motions, but deep down in your heart you don't love Me the way you used to. You have lost the burning desire you once had when you were first saved. Where is the passion to know Me, to delve into My Word and develop an intimate relationship with Me?

Then Jesus tells the church how to rekindle their first love—by doing "...*the works you did at first*"(v.5). It's a message every couple needs to hear and put into practice.

A Better Plan

Do you remember the thrill and excitement when you first fell in love? How you would linger on the phone for hours—and when you were together you couldn't keep your hands off each other? If you were apart, you ran to the post box every hour impatiently waiting for a letter to arrive.

Christ is reminding us, "Remember the height from which you have fallen— when things were at their peak."

Even more important, He assures us this love can be aroused and renewed once again.

One of the foremost lies Satan plants into the minds of husbands and wives is that after you have been married for awhile, feelings are automatically going to dim and become mundane. The devil wants you to believe it's *normal* to start fighting and faultfinding.

Christ has designed a far better plan. After asking you to recall what it was like when you first fell in love, and to look at your present situation, He doesn't casually suggest, "Do the best you can?"

No. Instead, He simply tells you to *"...repent"* (v.5).

This means you make a 180-degree turn and repeat your *"first works"* over again (v.5 KJV).

In the congregation at Ephesus, the people lost their original love by becoming so preoccupied with church activities they forgot about ministry.

Remember, Repent, Do!

The word "repent" means to *turn around*—not to just feel sorry for your actions. You return to the place you once knew and start doing those things again.

You may say, "Dan, I just don't feel like going back to those days."

The Lord didn't tell you to "feel" anything. He instructed you to (1) to remember, (2) to repent and (3) to do.

Don't wait till you *feel* romantic to become romantic. Let me offer this word of advice: It's easier to act your way into a new way of feeling than to feel your way into a new way of acting!

The Four "A's"

Here are four essential ingredients which will help ignite and rekindle the romance of your first love:

INGREDIENT # 1: ATTENTION

I vividly remember when Anna and I first met. She was a cheerleader in high school. At a pep rally, I looked over at her, dressed in her cute outfit, and thought, "This is the best looking 15-year old girl I've ever laid my eyes on."

From that moment on I began paying close attention —and soon found out she was also keeping her eye on me!

The Bible tells us not to be self-absorbed, but to show genuine interest in others (Philippians 2:4). However, as the years pass, our focus is diverted and we find ourselves using phrases such as, "What was it you said?" Or, "Repeat that again."

As a parent you always know when a member of the opposite sex begins paying attention to your teenager. Suddenly they start using deodorant and brush their teeth without you reminding them!

Keep it Fresh

Have you ever caught yourself daydreaming over your spouse? Maybe it was a tender comment he or she made, the way they laughed or the conversation you had at dinner last night. Perhaps it's time to make a phone call and say, "I just wanted to let you know I love you." This demonstrates to your partner you are still paying attention.

When was the last time you were walking together and you instinctively reached over and held the hand of your spouse?

This act may seem minor, but the implication is major.

Keep it Fresh and Focused

There are two reasons we can lose our attention:

First: The newness wears off.

Think of the excitement when you purchase a new car. You wash it every week, wipe off fingermarks with your sleeve, and the kids can't go for a ride if there's dirt on their shoes.

After a couple of months, things change. Now there are Taco Bell bags littering the back seat and the dog, dirty paws and all, jumps right in when it's time to visit the vet.

As individuals, our newness also wears thin. Your mate is constantly changing—and does not remain in the same place spiritually, physically or intellectually they were last year. Are you aware of these subtle changes? Are you paying close attention?

Second: Our objectives can make us oblivious to the needs of others.

My dad was a totally organized and single-minded individual. I can still remember him telling us kids before we left on a family vacation, "There are two things we are going to do tomorrow before we leave. The gas tank will be full and your bladders will be empty. And we will not stop until the gas tank is empty and your bladders are full!"

We got the message!

"What's Happening Here?"

If matrimony is a man's goal, he will start behaving in a way completely foreign to him. For example, he will go to a bookstore and actually pay money for a book of poetry—or happily purchase an expensive bouquet of red roses. Yet, when the objective is reached and the rings have been exchanged, he moves on to his next project—providing for his wife and family.

When this transition takes place, suddenly he's not so attentive to the woman he courted. Before long, the wife thinks, "What's happening here? Why is he changing?"

Christ is asking us to return to our first love, and we must be obedient to His commands if our marriage is to succeed.

INGREDIENT #2: AFFIRMATION

Every time you express confidence in your partner you are engaged in emotional intimacy. Scripture tells us, *"Love each other with genuine affection, and take delight in honoring each other"* (Romans 12:10). We are to, *"...encourage each other and build each other up"* (1 Thessalonians 5:11).

The shortest path to returning romance to your marriage is to once again generously affirm and admire the strengths of your spouse rather than focusing on the weaknesses. The same devotion and attitude you showed *before* the wedding should be your behavior now.

If you have a "pet" name for your husband or wife, use it often.

Recently I read a list of the "Top 10 Pet Names for a Spouse." Here are the terms of endearment in reverse order—with the most used name last.

10. Precious (or Beautiful)
9. Angel
8. Punkin
7. Sugar
6. Darling
5. Lover
4. Dear
3. Sweetheart
2. Baby
1. Honey

Which do you use—or do you have an affectionate nickname even more special?

Advice from an Attorney

There is tremendous power in affirmation and absolutely zero merit in tearing another person down. You say, "I can't forgive and forget; you don't know what he did." Or, "You have no idea how hateful she is acting." No I don't, but throwing verbal darts doesn't solve the problem; it only provokes and prolongs the agony of what took place.

I heard the true story of a woman who met with an attorney because she hated her husband with a passion and wanted a divorce. She told the lawyer, "I've given him the best years of my life. I not only want to divorce him, I want you to help me hurt him so deeply he will never ever forget how he has ignored me all these years."

The bitter woman went on to explain how her husband had placed his career ahead of their relationship—and she felt alone and neglected."

The attorney thought for a few moments and replied, "I have a plan which will accomplish exactly what you want."

"What is it?" she wanted to know.

He said, "For the next two or three weeks, while I

am getting all the paperwork together, I want you to go home and start complimenting your husband. Continually brag on everything he does. Tell him how great he is."

"Why in the world would I want to do that?" she responded, rather confused.

"Because," replied the lawyer, "when you do, he hopefully will fall in love with you all over again—and when we hit him with the divorce papers he will be absolutely devastated. He will be hurt more than you can ever imagine!"

As this was her goal, she did exactly as he suggested. She began to feed his ego, showering him with praise—for the way he provided for the family, how he cared for the kids and was successful in his career.

Before long, the man was returning the praise. When he sat down at the dinner table, he told her, "You're a gourmet cook." And when they went out one evening, he whispered, "You really know how to dress."

Three weeks later, the woman called the attorney and exclaimed, "Your plan worked like a charm!"

"Good," he responded, "when are we going to file the papers?"

"We're not," she told him with excitement mounting in her voice. "Cancel the divorce. We have both fallen in love all over again!"

---------- ⊖ ----------
*This was a living testimony
to the miracle of affirmation.*

INGREDIENT # 3: AFFECTION

The first sporting event mentioned in the Bible is described in Genesis 26:8 where we read, *"Isaac was sporting with Rebekah his wife."*

The word "sporting" in Hebrew means "to caress playfully or to fondle."

What's great about this activity is it can be played year around, regardless of the weather. If it's snowing outside we can light a fire, enjoy some hot chocolate and hug the partner we love.

Men, let me offer this word of advice. If the only affection you give your wife is to signal you are ready for sex, your advances will eventually be rebuffed.

There is a huge difference between foreplay and affection. Your wife has a basic need for non-sexual touching, tenderness and caressing.

A national newspaper columnist asked readers to

respond to this question: "If you had to choose between being held tenderly or sexual intimacy, which would you prefer?"

Seventy-seven percent said they'd choose "being held."

Please understand, tenderness and affection in the life of a woman is just as important as sexual fulfillment is to a man.

INGREDIENT # 4: ADVENTURE

If your spouse were asked to describe you to a total stranger, what words would be used? Exciting? Boring? Unpredictable? Stimulating? Dull? Adventurous? A sour-puss? A ball of fire?"

As a husband, when was the last time you surprised your wife with an "off the wall" escapade?

Let me offer a suggestion. On the next Saturday the weatherman predicts it's going to be a beautiful day, get up that morning and tell your wife, "Look, whatever you planned to do today, forget about it. Let's go for a drive."

If you have kids, arrange for a babysitter or take

them to Aunt Suzy's. You're about to experience what I call a "Hidden Picnic!"

In the trunk of the car you've already packed the sandwiches and a dessert. The soft drinks are in a cooler.

Next, you drive to a romantic spot you've carefully picked out, spread a blanket, lay out the picnic supplies, start playing her favorite songs on a portable CD and fondly whisper, "Honey, this day is just for you!"

Enjoy!

Are you committed to making the effort to rekindle the romance in your marriage? With God's help it will happen through Attention, Affirmation, Affection and Adventure.

Our Heavenly Father *"...richly provides us with everything for our enjoyment"* (1 Timothy 6:17 NIV). This includes the "one and only" He has brought into your life.

Your love song need never end!

Chapter Eight

The Fidelity Factor

I heard the story about a make-believe televison show produced in Southern Califorina which perhaps you can visualize yourself being part of.

You and your family are visiting and just happen to get tickets—but you have no idea what the show is about.

Suddenly, the host announces, "Today's prize is the largest amount we've ever given away. The winner is going to receive, not $1 million, $5 million...but someone is going to walk out of here ten million dollars richer!"

A hush falls over the studio as the contestant's name is called out—and, to your surprise, it's you! Two hostesses escort you to the stage and the announcer asks, "Are you ready to play the game?"

"Sure," you nervously reply.

The curtain opens and there is a wheelbarrow filled with more cash than you have ever seen before. "Go ahead and run your hands through it," smiles the congenial host. And you do!

Out in the audience your kids are jumping up and down and your spouse is giving you two thumbs up!

"It can be all yours," he continues. "All you have to do is answer the question, 'What is your price?' If you agree on one condition, the money is yours!"

Would You?

You are thinking, "$10 million. Yes, I can do this!" And your mind races, thinking of what you will do with the money. Set up your retirement, buy your dream home, give to your church and help the needy.

"Let's get started," continues the host. I'm going to read the list and you tell me which of these eight things you would do to receive the grand prize."

One: Put your children up for adoption.
Two: Become a prostitute for a week.
Three: Give up your American citizenship.
Four: Abandon your religious faith.
Five: Leave your family.
Six: Kill a stranger.
Seven: Have a sex-change operation.
Eight: Change your race.

The Real Results

Before you make your decision, the announcer tells you the results of a national survey where people were actually given the same choices and allowed to reply anonymously:

- Twenty-five percent would leave their family.
- Twenty-five percent would abandon their faith.
- Twenty-three percent would become a prostitute for a week.
- Sixteen percent would forfeit their American citizenship.

- Six percent would change their race.
- Four percent would have a sex change operation.
- Three percent would put their children up for adoption.
- An astonishing seven percent would murder for the money!

Here's the most amazing fact: two-thirds of those polled would agree to at least one (and many several) of the options.

Although this game is a figment of some producer's imagination, is there a trade you would make for a cash-laden wheelbarrow?

The Urge to Roam

In reading this story you may think, "How ridiculous! I wouldn't break any laws of man or God. I'd never do any of those things for money!"

Well, just think of the behavior of people where no dollars are involved. Statistics support the fact that approximately half of all married men have had an extramarital affair—and 30 percent of married women.

Redbook Magazine reports that of spouses who work outside the home, the number of cheating women rises to 46 percent.

Causes of marital infidelity vary as much as the personalities who are involved.

During the time I was working on my master's degree and doctorate, we were also counseling those who were experiencing conflict in their marriages—as many as four and five couples per day would come to our office.

As I talked with spouses who had been unfaithful in their marriage, a pattern began to emerge. Over time I drew some conclusions concerning *why* one of the partners (and sometimes both) begin to roam.

Earlier in this book we discussed one major cause: the lack of *fun* in the relationship. But there are also other reasons.

Please understand, I don't wish to justify infidelity, only to help explain the underlying causes of why spouses cheat.

Still Adolescent?

Many married people are unfaithful because of emotional immaturity.

Most parents fear adolescence in their sons and daughters as much as they do childhood disease. It is a time of rapidly changing relationships, agonizing peer pressure and questions concerning one's identity, and the future. This stage is not meant to be permanent, rather it is a bridge between dependency of childhood and his or her dependency as an adult.

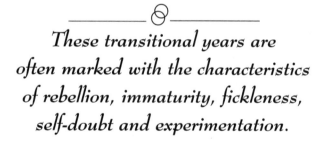

These transitional years are often marked with the characteristics of rebellion, immaturity, fickleness, self-doubt and experimentation.

Unfortunately, some people in their 30s, 40s and even 50s are still juvenile in their behavior. Furthermore, instead of marriage being a "last best chance" to grow up, it becomes a reflector of those immaturities.

The "Workaholic"

When I was a teenager and had just surrendered my life to preach the Gospel, there was an associate pastor at our church who was greatly admired. He was a jack-of-all-trades kind of guy who could sing, play musical instruments and preach. Even more, he had earned his pilot's license, could fix the plumbing or repair a car. To top it off, he loved people—and they loved him in return.

When he felt led to move to another city and start a church, our congregation wholeheartedly supported him, along with his beautiful wife and two outstanding teenage sons. They all admired him and cherished the ground he walked on.

Starting with a few people in their home, the fledgling church soon grew to several hundred people—with a Christian school of over 800.

Sadly, this gifted pastor began to believe his own press and thought he was invincible—that nothing could touch him. He was convinced he was protected by a shield because God was obviously blessing his ministry.

Before long, he hired a personal secretary and they

were both workaholics—even spending late hours at the office together.

One of the leaders of the church became concerned and quietly approached him, advising, "Pastor, you need to watch yourself when it involves working after hours. Your car and her car being on the church property late at night doesn't look good. And it may be a temptation you need to guard against."

"Don't worry," the pastor replied, "I can handle this."

However, it wasn't long until he set up a security system in his offices that would cause a light to go on if anyone entered the hallway area. In addition, he installed a soundproof door on his office.

Missing the Clues

People didn't really want to think the worst, yet, an extramarital affair had been taking place for 18 months before his wife finally learned the truth and, brokenhearted, left with the sons.

During this sad time, the church began to dwindle—and I am sorry to say that today it no longer exists.

He proudly boasted, "I can handle this," but the

Bible says, *"Pride leads to disgrace"* (Proverbs 11:2).

Looking back on this man's life, there were clues of his character flaws. His flirtatious nature around women should have set off red flags.

Bolstering Self-Esteem

Dr. Frank Minirth of the Minirth-Meier Clinic observes, "People have affairs, not because they have fallen in love with other people. It is because they feel inferior, and having someone of the other sex fall in love with them makes them feel temporarily significant."

The more insecure individuals are the more affairs they are likely to have—to bolster their self-esteem.

An emotionally mature person has a realistic sense of his or her own weaknesses.

Solving Strife

Another significant cause for infidelity is unresolved conflicts. The reality of tension in the intimacy of marriage is inevitable. It *will* happen.

This is why Scripture warns, *"...don't sin by letting*

anger control you" (Ephesians 4:26). Notice, it does not say, "Anger is a sin," rather, we are told not to sin when we are angry—which we do when we hold onto the reason for our wrath. What is the biblical solution, *"Don't let the sun go down while you are still angry, for anger gives a foothold to the devil"* (vv.26-27).

Who Does the Chores?

A major source of friction in many households is the question of who is going to perform a particular chore.

I laughed when I read the answers to a national survey where women were asked, "Would you rather watch a man dance naked or have him wash the dishes?"

An amazing 61 percent answered, "wash the dishes."

They were also questioned whether they would prefer a man who looked like Danny DeVito help with the chores around the house—or one who resembled Robert Redford, yet did no housework.

Forty-three percent chose Danny DeVito!

In another study of 155 married adults, 42 percent of men and 35 percent of women argued over household chores—and 14 percent of the men admitted they had botched an assignment to get out of doing the same task again!

Crashing and Smashing!

In the home where I grew up there were four males and two females living under the same roof. My mother was a CPA and my sister became the financial controller of a rather large company. They were accountants and everything was precise—their hair and nails were always properly groomed and they both exuded style and professionalism.

My mother and sister sharpened their expertise by reading, listening, assessing and applying.

What about the four guys—dad, my older and younger brothers, and me? That's another story. As I like to say, "Men learn and process information by *breaking* things!"

As boys, we only worry over what happens *after* we crash or smash an object, but our methods don't seem to change much when we are older.

I asked one man who owned an all-terrain vehicle, "How's your ATV?"

"It's running great, he answered, "but I'm going to

take it apart next week."

"What's the problem?" I wanted to know.

"Oh, nothing," he answered, "I just like putting it back together."

You see, it's the nature of many men to learn through the tearing-apart and fixing routine. That's how we discover how things work!

In many cases, this is how men approach relationships—by breaking them down to see what makes them tick.

Let me illustrate what I mean. A gentleman stopped by my office and said, "Pastor, I think I've really botched things at home and I'm not sure my wife will forgive me."

At first, the matter didn't seem to be of major consequence, until he confided, "Actually, it's the third time I have done this. She's forgiven me before, but I just wanted to test her to see how far I could go before she blew a fuse. I considered it a learning process."

Women, try to understand where your mate is coming from. Those "Tinker Toys" they played with as a child sometimes resurface in married life—and you may be the one they are tinkering with!

The Wages of Wandering

The man who believes, "If I just had another woman, I'd be happy" is living in a fool's paradise.

―――――― ⊗ ――――――
I have counseled men who had <u>three</u> women on the side and they were living in absolutely misery.

Solomon had 700 wives and 300 concubines, but *"...they* [turned] *his heart away from the Lord"* (1 Kings 11:3).

Let me share with you a story about a friend I've known all my life who, at the age of 19, got a girl pregnant and they married. He didn't take care of his family financially and she eventually left him. His friends were far more important—and soon he found himself involved with alcohol and drugs. Then he met a woman in a local bar and fathered another child.

Since they were both running around on each other, this marriage lasted only a year or two.

Next, he married for the third time—taking care of his second wife's child plus those from his current marriage.

However, thank God, there is a positive ending to this story. It took him until the age of 32 before he realized that if he didn't give his heart to the Lord and have a spiritual transformation, there would never be any hope for his future. He and his family began attending church and through God's redeeming grace, found the true meaning of love.

Move Toward the Top

Let me remind you there is a divine triangle in any successful marriage—the husband, the wife and the top of the apex represents God and His love.

As the spouses move closer to the top, they also draw closer to each other. If you fail to recognize this truth, your marriage will be in jeopardy—or you will be so unhappy you *wish* it would fail!

―――――― ⊘ ――――――
The partner who glibly passes the buck, saying, "I'll let him (or her) do the spiritual thing," misses the point.

When this happens, the distance between the two in the bottom part of the triangle remains the same.

Each of you has a responsibility to move toward God. When you do, you will feel His presence and the quickening of the Holy Spirit in your relationship. This is your source of guidance to become the kind of partner the Lord intends for you to be.

Let the Healing Begin

Don't be foolish enough to float through life believing you are immune from the temptation of extramarital affairs. We *all* have to protect ourselves from this trap of Satan.

I have counseled far too many who say, "You don't know how lonely I am." Or, "I'm going through a mid-life crisis." These must never be excuses.

If you have experienced the pain of admitting an

infidelity to your spouse, please know that through the process of your forgiveness, and God's, the healing can begin. Your marriage is worth fighting for—and can be stronger from this day forward than it has ever been.

I pray you will do your part to help make your future everything your Heavenly Father has planned.

Chapter Nine

Affair-Proof Your Marriage

After spending many years of my youth in Texas, I know a little about country music—and when you listen to the lyrics of the songs, it's no wonder so many spouses are running around on their mates!

The titles alone reflect the sad state of our society:

- "Your Cheatin' Heart"—Hank Williams
- "One Has My Name, The Other Has My Heart"—Jimmy Wakely
- "Back Street Affair"—Webb Pierce

It still amazes me that people who have been raised in Christian homes and have been exposed to Scripture all their lives willfully choose to ignore one of the Ten

Commandments: *"You must not commit adultery"* (Exodus 20:14).

Still, husbands and wives by the millions break their marriage vows—allowing their sexual urges to have dominion over commitment and common sense. Sooner or later, there will be a heavy price to pay. As the writer of Proverbs asks, *"Can a man scoop a flame into his lap and not have his clothes catch on fire? Can he walk on hot coals and not blister his feet? So it is with the man who sleeps with another man's wife. He who embraces her will not go unpunished"* (Proverbs 6:27-29).

Before we discuss how to protect your marriage from a disastrous affair, let's look at what God has to say on the role of sex—and why our faithfulness is absolutely essential.

Naked—But Not Ashamed

In Genesis we read how the Creator decided it was not good for man to be alone, *"So the Lord God caused the man to fall into a deep sleep. While the man slept, the Lord God took out one of the man's ribs and closed up the opening. Then the Lord God made a woman* from the rib, and he brought her to the man. 'At last!' the man exclaimed. 'This one is bone from my bone, and flesh from my flesh! She will be called "woman," because she was taken from 'man'"* (Genesis 2:21-23).

Scripture continues, *"This explains why a man leaves his father and mother and is joined to his wife, and the two are united into one. Now the man and his wife were both naked, but they felt no shame"* (vv.25-26).

We later read that Adam "knew" Eve—or, *"...Adam had sexual relations with his wife, Eve, and she became pregnant"* (Genesis 4:1).

Why Sex?

Since God invented sex, we should not be ashamed to discuss what He was not embarrassed to create.

―――――― ✆ ――――――
*When the Creator made you,
He didn't make certain parts of your body
"bad" and other parts "good."*

All of your physical being is virtuous in His sight

—including your sexual organs: *"So honor God with your body"* (1 Corinthians 6:20).

Our Heavenly Father invented sex for three reasons:

First: To promote unity.

In both the Old and New Testaments we read how two individuals are to become one (Genesis 2:24; Ephesians 5:31).

When words are no longer adequate to express our innermost feelings, intimate relations become a means of communication.

Through sex we are united in both a physical experience and an emotional reality.

Second: To provide pleasure.

The Bible tells us marital intimacy should be mutually enjoyable. *"The husband should fulfill his wife's sexual needs, and the wife should fulfill her husband's needs."* (1 Corinthians 7:3).

All aspects of our lives are to be filled with the Spirit—and two of these are *love* and *joy* (Galatians 5:22).

Since the Lord blessed you with a spouse for your pleasure (Proverbs 5:18), you have a lifetime of happiness waiting ahead.

Third: To produce children.

God's directive to *"Be fruitful and multiply"* (Genesis 1:22) is often one of the few commands we keep. For many couples, it is the *only* reason.

Instead of delight and pleasure there is often anger, frustration, hurt and misunderstanding.

Minimize the Opportunities for Temptation

The allure of adultery can surface at any stage of marriage—from the honeymoon hotel to the retirement home. And those who believe they are immune to the problem are often the first to stumble.

The apostle Paul writes, *"If you think you are standing strong, be careful not to fall. The temptations in your life are no different from what others experience"* (1 Corinthians 10:12-13).

When are married people most vulnerable to temptation? From my counseling sessions, I have learned it is when they are bored, burdened or lonely. This also occurs when they have a deep-seated longing to be held and caressed—and are not receiving this affection at home.

In some instances they are looking for an escape from the pressure and responsibilities of life. Yet, they don't realize how adultery can result in far greater stress.

If you truly desire to build a barrier against even the remote possibility of infidelity, consider these four steps.

1. Recognize the dangers of a business trip.

I realize many men—and women—are required to travel and be separated from their families in order to make a living. But I also know the temptations which can be lurking during a road trip.

Long hours are usually involved and conversations with business associates of the opposite sex seem inevitable.

In the evening, since you are away from your family, loneliness can easily creep in. Just a lingering gaze or a gentle squeeze of the arm can suddenly trigger unexpected responses. You suddenly become open and extremely vulnerable.

On such trips, you need to minimize the opportunities for seduction.

Extramarital affairs don't normally began with a stranger, they start with a friend —a person you are already acquainted with.

2. Shun the appearance of impropriety.

As a husband, take every precaution against scheduling business luncheons where only you and a woman are present. You say, "Pastor, you don't understand. In my line of work, it's often unavoidable."

Take another guest with you or make some alternate arrangement. Remember, Scripture tells us, *"Avoid the very appearance of evil"* (1 Thessalonians 5:22 KJV).

As a cautious friend once told me, "I make it a personal policy never to be alone in a car with a woman who is not my wife—and that includes job-related travel. He added, "How would it look if the car broke down and we had to spend the night in another part of the state? Or, what if we were involved in a fatal car accident? How would my family handle the inevitable questions?"

3. Avoid spending time with those who don't hold the vows of marriage in high priority.

Let's face facts. In the average secular office or factory plenty of flirting takes place, and there are dozens of ways people send off signals they are available—whether married or unmarried.

In work environments there are individuals who, during a coffee break or at lunch, take great delight in bragging about their sexual exploits or extramarital affairs. From years of counseling, I know these conversations take place.

You may comment, "Sure, people talk, but I'm stronger than that. It doesn't affect me."

Yes, it certainly does. God's Word declares, *"... "bad company corrupts good character"* (1 Corinthians 15:33).

4. If you ever feel attracted to an individual in the slightest sexual way, make it a point to avoid them.

Married or not, you are going to be drawn to others you find physically or emotionally appealing.

This may come as a shocker to some, but there are other men and women in this world more attractive than you!

Anna and I were watching a Sylvester Stallone movie—it was one where he couldn't seem to keep his shirt on. About the third time this happened, my wife leaned over to me and whispered, "Honey, I've never really been attracted to well-built men!"

Ouch! That really made me feel great!

Seriously, if you are ever in the presence of a person to whom you feel drawn—or feel vibes coming from the other individual toward you—take the initiative to stop it before it begins. How? Start by sending a strong signal concerning your relationship with your spouse.

For example, when the time is right, pull out your wallet and say, "Let me show you a picture of my wife and kids."

By this very act you are communicating, "Don't even think about it!"

Personal Prudence

Perhaps you are thinking, "Dan, this is good advice for others, but what about you? What rules do you set for your own behavior?"

When I have to speak at a conference away from home, I take certain precautions.

First, I try to have somebody accompany me. If Anna can't travel at the time, I do my best to take one of my staff members. If this is not possible, I try to make sure there is a pastor or long-term friend in that city and let him occupy my time and attention.

Next, in my briefcase, I pack a picture of my wife and kids. When I unpack at the hotel, the first thing I do is place it on top of the television or desk. It's a constant visual reminder of who I have waiting for me at home.

If there is a "blue" channel or pay-per-view on the TV, I phone the front desk and ask them to block it. You say, "Wait a minute. As a pastor, are you telling me you have a problem with X-rated movies?"

No, I don't, but in addition to removing the slightest temptation, I want it on record that it would be impossible for me to view such material.

Wherever possible, I make sure to use a credit card which reads, "Rev. Daniel C. Hooper," because I am proud to be a minister of the Gospel and it lets others know certain standards are expected of me. I am a representative of the Lord Jesus Christ and do not want anything to jeopardize my reputation.

At our church we have specific standards for our staff. There are to be no lunches where an employee is to be alone with a member of the opposite sex, unless it is their spouse. In addition, no counseling sessions between a male and female are to take place when there is no one else on the property.

"Not Now!"

A woman once made this statement to a marriage counselor: "When it came to intimacy and sex, all my life I was told, 'No, No, No.' Then, after a 30-minute wedding ceremony, a ring and a piece of paper, I was told, 'Yes, Yes, Yes!'"

Then she added, "To be honest, it was really difficult for me to make the mental switch so quickly."

This is why, when it comes to explaining sex to our children, instead of simply saying "No," we need to emphasize, "Not now."

Information and knowledge concerning intimacy

needs to be discussed in the home, but make certain you send the right message. Discuss the fact that sex is a gift which is reserved for a husband and wife, and is not to be experimented with by teenagers.

Sex outside of marriage can result in complications which are absolutely irreversible. This is why it must be a gift we <u>anticipate</u>—not practice in which we <u>participate</u> before marriage.

I still laugh when I remember the night my wife and I were in a car with a young couple who were engaged. Our discussion that evening focused on the Second Coming of Christ. They both confessed they had prayed, "Lord, please don't return until we get married and enjoy our honeymoon!"

Maintain an Affair at Home

The most effective way to protect yourself from an extramarital sexual relationship is to plan to have a lifelong affair under your own roof!

If you make the grass greener at home, everything else will pale in comparison!

Let me offer these five keys to help make this a reality:

KEY #1: HAVE THE RIGHT ATTITUDE ABOUT SEX

In our media-driven culture, it's easy to draw the wrong conclusions concerning intimate relationships.

If a husband or wife believes their spouse is going to respond to their sexual advances the same way it is portrayed by Hollywood, they are in for quite a disappointment.

What we see emblazoned on the big screen is called "acting"—not reality. Yet, we carry these images and ideas with us into a marriage. For example, a young man may conclude, "If I just kiss her on her neck, it will drive her crazy!"

For some women, however, this drives them nuts!

Another cause of distorted sexual attitudes is that

many parents, feeling inadequate, are reluctant to tell their children one word about sex. It is an uncomfortable, and often taboo, subject.

Wrong attitudes can also surface from uninformed experiences—often the result of peer pressure which causes teens to experiment with sex.

So where do we turn to find the right answer concerning intimate relationships? We open the pages of God's Word.

Lovemaking between a husband and wife is an honorable activity. *"Since everything God created is good, we should not reject any of it but receive it with thanks"* (1 Timothy 4:4).

KEY #2: BRING SOME EXCITEMENT TO THE BEDROOM

For many couples, their sex life is totally predictable. It's the same time, the same place the same routine. At exactly 9:00 P.M., Harry leaps from the bathroom looking like a beached whale with a big grin on his face!

Sally is waiting in bed—with her hair looking like an explosion in a steel-wool factory! She is still wearing the same robe she's had for years and hasn't bothered to wipe off the wrinkle cream she lathers her face with each evening.

Harry enters the bed with all the grace and finesse of a John Deere tractor!

This is not intimacy or lovemaking, it's just sex—and we wonder why it isn't exciting anymore.

Key #3: Learn How to Please your Partner

A husband and wife who were celebrating their 50th wedding anniversary told me, "We had been married for 15 years before we had a clue concerning what a mutually satisfying sexual relationship is all about."

The gentleman commented, "I didn't know and she couldn't tell me. So we struggled through many years before we learned how to please each other."

From a number of studies we learn that from stimulation to orgasm, the average time for a man is between two and three minutes. For a woman, however, it takes 12 to14 minutes.

This should tell you that for sex to be mutually enjoyable and satisfying, there has to be compromise.

As I often say, "Men are like a light switch and women more like a crockpot."

Men, relax and enjoy. Don't be in such a hurry!

Key #4: Make the Right Adjustments

Research reveals that the average couple takes up to six years to adjust to a mutually satisfying sexual relationship. Only 12 percent make the necessary adjustments within the first year and 10 percent take up to 20 years! So don't give up.

It is mutual!

"The wife gives authority over her body to her husband, and the husband gives authority over his body to his wife."
– 1 Corinthians 7:4

In today's hectic world, we all face the problems of time, schedule and energy. This is why I recommend you plan to have a balanced "diet" in your sex life:

- There are times when you and your spouse may have only five minutes—a snack!

- On other occasions you may have 25 or 30 minutes—a meal!
- If you can set aside 45 minutes or longer —now that's a banquet!

Speaking on this subject to a group of men, I smiled and told them, "Remember, wives shall not live by snacks alone!"

If just a fleeting encounter is all you ever have to offer, you're causing your wife to become emotionally malnourished.

Key #4: Create the Right Atmosphere

How can we turn the bedroom from a battleground into a playground?

The perfect "ambiance" is not nearly as important to a man as it is for a woman. You could have a house full of guests, but some men would like to hurry them out the door because he is ready "right now." While a woman must have time to prepare herself for sexual intimacy.

Males are stimulated visually—they see what they want. Females, however, are aroused emotionally and need the atmosphere of affection which takes place over a longer period of time.

Learn the Techniques

It's a myth to believe lovemaking "just comes naturally." Wrong! It is a skill which must be learned.

To gain a better insight into the techniques of giving and receiving love, read the romantic adventures recorded in the Song of Solomon. Here are just a few:

- **Compliment your spouse.**
  "How beautiful you are, my darling, how beautiful! Your eyes are like doves" (Song of Solomon 1:15).
- **Prepare your body for romance.**
  "The king is lying on his couch, enchanted by the fragrance of my perfume" (Song of Solomon 1:12).
- **Keep intimate moments private.**
  "The king has brought me into his bedroom" (Song of Solomon 1:4).

- **Learn the art of intimate talk.**
  "Kiss me and kiss me again, for your love is sweeter than wine" (Song of Solomon 1:2).
- **Express your total commitment to each other.**
  "Place me like a seal over your heart, like a seal on your arm. For love is as strong as death, its jealousy as enduring as the grave" (Song of Solomon 8:6).

Since lovemaking involves our time, attention and practice, go out of your way to make the encounter special. I recommend now-and-again taking a one-night, romantic, mini-vacation at a local hotel. You complain, "We can't afford that." Well remember, in most cases, a night out is cheaper than a one hour session with a psychologist or marriage counselor!

KEY#5: MAKE A COMMITMENT TO GOD'S STANDARD

David asks, *"How can a young person stay pure?"* (Psalm 119:9). He then gives the answer to his own question: *"By obeying your word"* (v.9).

Until you accept what the Lord presents as His standard for your life, you will be lacking in this area.

I fiercely guard the fidelity of my marriage like a soldier protects his post. I do not want to ever bring reproach or pain to my church, my wife or my children.

The number one reason, however, is because I love the Lord with all my heart and He says, "Do not!" His command is good enough for me.

Scripture tells us, *"Give honor to marriage, and remain faithful to one another in marriage. God will surely judge people who are immoral and those who commit adultery"* (Hebrews 13:4).

This is a divine law by which we are to live.

The Path to Restoration

The "wages" of adultery are severe. *"For the lips of an immoral woman are as sweet as honey, and her mouth is smoother than oil. But in the end she is as* bitter as poison, as dangerous as a double-edged sword"* (Proverbs 5:3-4).

David strayed from the path and suffered the consequences. As he describes his experience, *"When I refused to confess my sin, my body wasted away, and I groaned all day long. Day and night your hand of discipline was heavy on me. My strength evaporated like water in the summer heat"* (Psalm 32:3-4).

This brings us to the question, "If I *have* sinned and made a mistake in my marriage, how can I make things right?"

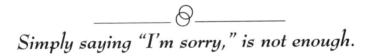

Simply saying "I'm sorry," is not enough.

You have to personally repent before God, humbly ask for the forgiveness of your spouse and make a total commitment from your heart and soul you will never, ever walk down this same path again.

Here's how David found divine restoration. *"Finally, I confessed all my sins to you and stopped trying to hide my guilt. I said to myself, 'I will confess my rebellion to the Lord.' And you forgave me! All my guilt is gone"* (v.5).

Praise God!

With the Lord's help, you will never have to endure the trauma caused by adultery. *"Drink water from your own well—share your love only with your wife. Why spill the water of your springs in the streets, having sex with just anyone? You should reserve it for yourselves. Never share it with strangers. Let your wife be a fountain of blessing for you"* (Proverbs 5: 15-18).

Take every step necessary to affair-proof your marriage.

Chapter Ten

A Prosperous Partnership

You may find this surprising, but I've always found it is easier for couples to discuss their personal intimate relationships than their finances. Yet, money—or the mismanagement of it—has been cited as the number one cause of marriage breakups in newlywed couples.

Sure, there may be other underlying problems, but money woes squeeze them to the surface. In fact, couples who start fighting over finances are often using the issue as a convenient "scapegoat" to hide what is *really* bothering them. Before long, however, the true source of their conflict will surface.

Apply the Right Principles

The only benefit I can think of for a "cash crunch"

in your marriage is that it may cause you to face reality—and devise a game plan to insure it never happens again. Complaining about the problem won't make it go away. You have to make a total commitment to change your habits.

It's much like standing in front of a mirror every morning being upset about your increasing weight. The only answer is to decide on a diet and exercise plan, then stick to it until you reach your goal.

The benefits of Double Play in your partnership —Joy and Abundance—are the result of understanding and applying God's divine directives.

Let me share seven principles that can help build a strong financial foundation for your marriage:

Principle #1: All Wealth Comes from God

We don't bring a bank account with us when we enter this world, and we certainly can't take our stocks and bonds to heaven when we leave.

Every ounce of gold or silver we are allowed to hold in our hand is on loan from our Heavenly Father. It was His from the beginning, and will be His for eternity.

As David proclaimed, *"Everything in the heavens*

and on earth is yours, O Lord, and this is your kingdom. We adore you as the one who is over all things. Wealth and honor come from you alone, for you rule over everything"* (1 Chronicles 29:11-12).

When we understand that wealth comes from above and belongs to God, we begin to realize we are merely *trustees* of what He allows us to have. Since He has placed this treasure in our care, we have an obligation to handle it wisely.

PRINCIPLE #2: GOD WANTS YOUR MARRIAGE TO FINANCIALLY PROSPER

Those who believe the Lord desires His children to live in poverty are not reading the same Bible I am! From Genesis to Revelation there is an undeniable message of blessing and favor. Satan may come to steal, kill and destroy, but the Lord declares, *"...I am come that they might have life, and that they might have it more abundantly"* (John 10:10 KJV).

―――――― ☙ ――――――
*The password which unlocks
God's safety deposit box of blessing
is spelled o-b-e-d-i-e-n-c-e.*

The Father's favor is not promised for *every* husband and wife, only those who obey His Word. For example, the psalmist tells us, *"How joyful are those who fear the Lord—all who follow his ways! You will enjoy the fruit of your labor. How joyful and prosperous you will be! Your wife will be like a fruitful grapevine, flourishing within your home. Your children will be like vigorous young olive trees as they sit around your table. That is the Lord's blessing for those who fear him"* (Psalm 28:1-4).

God has a history of sharing His abundance, but it is reserved for those who believe, trust and follow His commands.

PRINCIPLE #3: IF YOU EXPECT TO EAT, PLAN TO WORK

I've talked with couples whose finances were in a mess, yet they didn't seem the least concerned, "God will take care of us," they repeated again and again. In many cases they were living on handouts from friends and relatives rather than actively searching for employment.

Let me say this as clearly as I know how. God's

number one plan for your financial success is based on diligent work—by you!

Here is what Scripture declares:

- *"Work brings profit, but mere talk leads to poverty"* (Proverbs 14:23)
- *"Whatever your hand finds to do, do it with all your might"* (Ecclesiastes 9:10 NIV).
- *"If anyone will not work, neither shall he eat"* (2 Thessalonians 3:10 NKJV).

King Solomon gives us sound advice regarding labor and industry by calling our attention to one of the tiniest creatures on earth—the lowly ant. He says, *"Take a lesson from the ants, you lazybones. Learn from their ways and be wise! Even though they have no prince, governor, or ruler to make them work, they labor hard all summer, gathering food for the winter. But you, lazybones, how long will you sleep? When will you wake up? I want you to learn this lesson: A little extra sleep, a little more slumber, a little folding of the hands to rest—and poverty will pounce on you like a bandit; scarcity will attack you like an armed robber"* (Proverbs 6:6-11).

> *God isn't going to wave a heavenly wand over your marriage and say, "Be successful and live in abundance."*

Rather, the Bible declares, *"...the Lord your God will make you most prosperous in all the work of your hands"* (Deuteronomy 30:9 NIV).

In your Heavenly Father's sight, labor is a virtue.

Principle #4: Become Proficient in Personal Money Management

It still amazes me that students can graduate from college without ever having taken one course on how to control their finances.

Look at your marriage as an enterprise which requires a business plan—because it truly does. This is why the spouse who is going to handle the money in the home needs to enroll in a Personal Finance class. Even better, both the husband and wife should take the course together, so each can give well-informed input to the process.

- Do you know how to set up a workable budget?
- Can you analyze your income potential?
- Do you have the tools to evaluate your assets, liabilities and household cash flow?
- Can you properly evaluate how you are spending your time—to make your hours more productive?
- Are you and your spouse prepared to discuss financial decision making?

Don't allow your home to become a "Cash Court" where you are constantly judging each other's entries in the checkbook.

If you are stressed and upset over finances, it's a sure sign your money is managing you—rather than the other way around.

I've counseled with couples whose income was nearly $500,000 a year, yet they were dead broke and buried in debt. Why? Because they had no idea where their money was going?

In today's economic reality it is absolutely essential

for families to have a handle on their finances.

Principle #5: Obey God's Laws of Giving

In our home, tithing is a no-brainer! Returning ten percent of what God allows us to receive is not a suggestion from the Almighty—it's a command.

In the Word we find this question: *"Will a man rob God? Yet you have robbed Me! But you say, 'In what way have we robbed You?' In tithes and offerings. You are cursed with a curse, for you have robbed Me, even this whole nation. Bring all the tithes into the storehouse, that there may be food in My house"* (Malachi 3:8-10 NKJV).

However, this command is accompanied by a glorious promise. The Lord declares, *"Try Me now in this...*[and see] *if I will not open for you the windows of heaven and pour out for you such blessing that there will not be room enough to receive it* (v.10).

If you handed me $100 and asked, "Hold onto this until next Sunday, then give it back," I wouldn't suddenly start thinking how I could spend it. You see, the funds are yours, not mine.

God's money must be treated in exactly the same

way. His ten percent is not yours to do as you please—it belongs to Him and is not to be borrowed against.

The tithe is the Lord, and your offerings (given as you feel led) are presented *in addition.* I can assure you from personal experience, when you obey God through giving, your home will be blessed beyond measure.

Principle #6: Make a Commitment to Help Others

An "us and ours" mentality in marriage leads to self-centered danger. God intends for there to be a rhythm and flow to your partnership—and this includes regularly giving to those who have needs.

One of the most powerful parables ever shared by Jesus compares the Kingdom of Heaven to a wealthy landowner who was going on a long journey. Before leaving, he entrusted his money to three of his household staff for safekeeping until he returned.

While the man was gone, the servant who was given five bags of silver invested the money and earned five more. The one with two bags of silver also doubled his. *"But the servant who received the one bag of silver dug a hole in the ground and hid the master's money"* (Matthew 25:18).

When the owner returned and learned the great news of how the first two had increased his money, he was thrilled beyond words.

He exclaimed, *"Well done, my good and faithful servant. You have been faithful in handling this small amount, so now I will give you many more responsibilities. Let's celebrate together!"* (v.23).

What happened to the servant who hid his master's money? There was nothing but excuses: *"Master, I knew you were a harsh man…I was afraid I would lose your money, so I hid it in the earth. Look, here is your money back"* (v.24).

The owner was so upset at this *"wicked and lazy servant"* (v.26), he actually took the bag of silver and gave it to the one who had produced ten bags!

Here is the message the Lord wants us to grasp: *"To those who use well what they are given, even more will be given, and they will have an abundance. But from those who do nothing, even what little they have will be taken away"* (v.28).

The do-nothing servant was sentenced to lose everything.

"One of the Least"

The reason Jesus shared this example is to illustrate what will happen when He returns to earth again. Those who are willing to help others will be received into the Kingdom, and those who refuse will suffer the consequences. It is a lesson on how we are to give ourselves—and our material goods—to those in need.

Immediately following this parable, Jesus offered an eye-opening comparison.

———— ⊘ ————

Read these words of Christ carefully, then ask yourself, "Are we, as a married couple, living up to God's expectations?"

Jesus declares, *"...when the Son of Man comes in his glory, and all the angels with him, then he will sit upon his glorious throne. All the nations will be gathered in his presence, and he will separate them as a shepherd separates the sheep from the goats. He will place the sheep at his right hand and the goats at his left. Then the King will say to those on the right, 'Come, you who are blessed by my Father, inherit the Kingdom prepared for you from the foundation of the world. For I was hungry, and you fed me. I was thirsty, and you gave me a drink. I was a stranger, and you invited me into your home. I was naked, and you gave me clothing. I was sick, and you cared for me. I was in prison, and you visited me"* (vv.31-36).

Then Jesus explained how the righteous will reply, *"Lord, when did we ever see you hungry and feed you? Or thirsty and give you something to drink? Or a stranger and show you hospitality? Or naked and give you clothing? When did we ever see you sick or in prison, and visit you?"* (vv.37-39).

The King will tell them, *"I assure you, when you did it to one of the least of these my brothers and sisters, you were doing it to me!"* (v.40).

Turning to those on the left, the King will then say, *"Away with you, you cursed ones, into the eternal fire prepared for the Devil and his demons! For I was hungry, and you didn't feed me. I was thirsty, and you didn't give me anything to drink. I was a stranger, and you didn't invite me into your home. I was naked, and you gave me no clothing. I was sick and in prison, and you didn't visit me."* (vv.41-43).

Not quite understanding they will reply, *"'Lord, when did we ever see you hungry or thirsty or a stranger or naked or sick or in prison, and not help you?' And he will answer, 'I assure you, when you refused to help the least of these my brothers and sisters, you were refusing to help me.' And they will go away into eternal punishment, but the righteous will go into eternal life"* (vv.44-46).

Is giving to others worth the investment? The answer is clear, *"If you help the poor, you are lending to the Lord—and he will repay you!"* (Proverbs 19:17).

We should never "give to get" yet God always honors what flows from our heart. The Bible promises, *"Give, and it will be given to you. A good measure, pressed down, shaken together and running over, will be poured into your lap. For with the measure you use, it will be measured to you"* (Luke 6:38 NIV).

What a marvelous model for a prosperous marriage!

PRINCIPLE #7: NEVER FORGET THE TRUE SOURCE OF YOUR ABUNDANCE

When your portfolio is expanding and the price of your real estate holdings are skyrocketing, it's easy to brag to your friends, "Look what we've done!"

*Wait just a minute!
Who made you wealthy?*

Remember the warning Moses declared to the children of Israel: *"Beware that in your plenty you do not forget the Lord your God and disobey his commands, regulations, and laws. For when you have become full and prosperous and have built fine homes to live in, and when your flocks and herds have become very large and your silver and gold have multiplied along with everything else, that is the time to be careful. Do not become proud at that time and forget the Lord your God, who rescued you from slavery in the land of Egypt"* (Deuteronomy: 8:11-14).

Moses reminded them that the trials and miracles experienced in the wilderness were *"...to humble you and test you for your own good. He did it so you would never say to yourself, 'I have achieved this wealth with my own strength and energy.' Remember the Lord your God. He is the one who gives you power to be successful, in order to fulfill the covenant he confirmed to your ancestors"* (vv.16-18).

Hope for Your Future

Let God's anointed Word be your ultimate anchor.

As a couple, *"Study this Book of Instruction continually. Meditate on it day and night so you will be sure to obey everything written in it. Only then will you prosper and succeed in all you do"* (Joshua 1:8).

One of my "life" verses, which I claim for myself and for our marriage, is this declaration by my Creator, *"For I know the plans I have for you...plans to prosper you and not to harm you, plans to give you hope and a future"* (Jeremiah 29:11 NIV).

It is also God's promise of blessing and abundance for all of His children—including you.

FOR A COMPLETE LIST
OF PUBLICATIONS
AND MEDIA MATERIALS, OR TO SCHEDULE THE
AUTHOR FOR SPEAKING ENGAGEMENTS,
CONTACT:

DAN HOOPER
HOOPER MINISTRIES
765 24 ROAD
GRAND JUNCTION, CO 81505

PHONE: 970-245-7729